ONE STONE
REVOLUTION

ONE STONE REVOLUTION

THE UNTOLD STORY

Akibo Robinson

ISBN: 978-1-4834-2302-9 (sc)
ISBN: 978-1-4834-2301-2 (e)

Library of Congress Control Number: 2014921884

Lulu Publishing Services rev. date: 01/15/2015

CONTENTS

PREFACE

After a generation of one-party rule, just when the return to multi-party democracy was approved, Sierra Leone's military staged a coup d'état in 1992. A four-year period of constitutional violation ended in 1996, when the international community negotiated a return to civilian rule, with the Khaki Boys.

Peaceful elections were held and won by the Sierra Leone People's Party, one of the more than ten political parties contesting the elections. Constitutionality was scarcely restored in the small but resources-rich country when another military coup, more brutal than any other seen in Sierra Leone, dethroned the elected government on 25 May 1997. The rule of this junta was so brutal that many people became internally displaced with another batch of Sierra Leoneans fleeing into neighbouring countries and beyond.

I belonged to a group that travelled to Ghana with my family, by road through Guinea, at a time when disposable income was very much inadequate as all the banks were closed due to insecurity during the brutal reign of the Armed Forces Revolutionary Council (AFRC).

Travelling by road in Africa by all accounts is hazardous with many checkpoints, inhospitable surroundings, bad roads, etc. Notwithstanding the strides made by the Economic Commission for West African States (ECOWAS), there is much work remaining to achieve reasonable political and economic integration.

To say the least, the journey was hazardous, and it took five days from Conakry, the capital of Guinea, to Accra, Ghana, where we stayed for six months.

During our stay in Ghana, I decided to document all our travails by keeping a handwritten diary of events. Perhaps this activity was a means of relieving our impotence and frustration at being "unproductive" but living at the expense of friends who had no connections to our conflict. At the end of the conflict when we returned home, again after a hazardous journey, I decided to turn my diary into a story, which I showed to friends for their comments and advice. After much deliberation and soul searching, coupled with their advice, I decided to publish my own version and interpretation of the Sierra Leone conflict.

From a historical perspective, the thirteen chapters of the book show the central ugly, untold stories of the mayhem of the 25 May 1997 AFRC junta and the 6 January insane invasion of Freetown. These events are definitely dark with elements of the unique—that is to say, *heinous*—atrocities riding on the back of gross impolicy specially made in Sierra Leone and by Charles Taylor in Liberia to prey on the lives of Sierra Leoneans. At the same time, they constitute a form of the absolutely depraved, universal lower selves of mankind in wanton rampage.

This is a story that attempts to address the theme of the decline of our original national values and our national governance. It also recognises the various roles played by the international community, especially the sub-regional grouping of the ECOWAS in the conflict, but also decries the support given by some Sierra Leonean elite to the perpetrators of bestial acts against an innocent people.

The war has been over for more than a decade now, and supposedly, these demons have been laid to rest. The moot question is this: have we learnt our lesson?

ACKNOWLEDGEMENTS

Without the love and encouragement of my family and some friends, this book would not have been written. The original intention was to neither write nor publish a book. During the time of the coup and subsequent military junta rule, when my wife, my son, and I travelled to Ghana by road, I started keeping a diary of events, just to stay in touch with reality.

My appreciation and thanks go to the Thomas Tetteh family in Labone, Accra, who gave us succour for six months, without charge. Without the encouragement of my wife and son, the diary would not have manifested into a book. My thanks go especially to Mr Joseph Carpenter, who gave up his valuable time to substantially edit the manuscript. Similarly, I wish to recognise the advice, comments and reviews given and made by Dr Adjai Robinson and Mr Kenneth Osho. My appreciation also goes to my daughter for her artistic advice and design of the cover page.

I will be sorely remiss in my duty if I failed to recognise the valuable contribution made by Justice George Gelega-King. There is no doubt in my mind that without his constant guidance, the diary would never have been turned into a book.

Finally, the author takes responsibility for any deficiencies in the text.

CHAPTER 1

GENESIS

Sierra Leone, land of the free, is a small country blessed with a wealth of resources: gold, diamonds, iron, bauxite, rutile—you name it. And now there is a well-grounded prospect of rich oil exploitation. With all this wealth, one would expect our countrymen to have an enviable quality of life. Alas, what a misconception. Yes, the country is rich, but the people are poor. Repeatedly in recent times, Sierra Leone has been at the bottom of the United Nations Human Development Index (HDI). This paradox is a travesty. No reason can be advanced for the deleterious state of our country, save the lack of a visionary who offers good leadership free from corruption and self-seeking propensities.

Our country, which was under colonial rule for more than 150 years, discarded that yoke in the early 1960s. In colonialism, there was some good but also the bad and the ugly. The golden age of our country was not ushered in with the unlocking of this colonial yoke, yet it boasted one of the best and oldest universities in sub-Saharan Africa, which served the length and breadth of the continent. In those halcyon days, our country was known as the "Athens of West Africa," and we were proud to be countrymen. The establishment operated in an orderly and reliable fashion and was somewhat effective and efficient in the discharge of its functions. The dictates of the general orders, financial orders, etc. were observed such that invocations of the concepts of transparency and accountability were scarce in those days. Propriety came as second nature. Nobody saw the need for a toothless anti-corruption commission because the law was not yet an ass.

Honesty, integrity, diligence, and self-esteem were virtues to be desired and admired—attributes that many people strove to achieve.

A government of national unity led by the Sierra Leone People's Party (SLPP), whose symbol was the palm tree, took us to independence in April 1961, and the new country was happy to stand on its own legs, even though there was some dissent on an issue in the decolonization agreement. About midway through the decade of the sixties, the first prime minister suddenly received his home call. And then things started to go awry. There was severe jostling for leadership positions. The policy of patronage started creeping into the corridors of power. Corruption and sycophancy reared their ugly heads. The aggressive tussle for power became fractious with disgruntled opportunists deciding to go their own way. When sanity prevailed, the leadership of the palm tree became a family affair, as the prime ministership was kept in the family and in the person of Albert Margai.

Independence brought us political liberation from colonialism, but it did not bring true political freedom, not to mention economic and financial independence. These we did not have. Left to ourselves, we allowed all our wealth to be exploited by foreign interests at the expense of our downtrodden countrymen. Our natural resources, sad to say, are still being plundered by foreigners in collaboration with the higher echelons of our society. As one of my teachers used to say, "Come one, come all. Seats free. No collection." This disillusioning devilry, modern *harambee* as he calls it, is a dominant theme of the novel *Devil on the Cross* by the Kenyan writer Ngugi Wa Thiong'o.

Those of us who are old enough know that a balance-of-payments crisis is not novel. During his regime, Albert Margai once vowed in one of his political campaign speeches that he would demolish the opposition leader. And he envisioned a one-party state where he could indulge in his excesses. Through his greed and profligacy, he led us into our first economic crisis. To salvage the situation, the International Monetary Fund had to enter the fray and hand our country a rescue package underpinned by currency depreciation.

Those days were fraught with political intolerance. The press was gagged, and opposition leaders were in and out of jail all the time. After all the politicking and bullying, it was not a surprise that during the campaign for the next general elections, the opposition, All People's Congress (APC), the sun-party, trumpeted the ruling palm tree party's thirst for dictatorial rule. They used the one-party state philosophy as a weapon to discredit it. What came as a surprise to some and a shock to others was the opposition's victory at the polls in 1967. In the Africa of those days, that was anathema: an opposition party was never voted into power. In this case, the rulers were removed from office by the people through the power of the vote, not the gun.

Alas, this unique achievement was not allowed to stand, as the election results were annulled because of the proclivity of Margai. Instead of conceding defeat, he decided to invite a military junta to take over the reins of government. This was the presage of things to come, a repeated, tormenting threat to interfere in civilian governance by the military. Nevertheless, Sierra Leone was still unique. During that short period, our country had four different heads of state within a week. We had never seen the likes of it, nor will we ever see such occurrences in this lifetime. But that was not the worst.

Irony of ironies. When the dust finally settled after about fifteen months and the democratically elected government of Siaka Stevens was duly installed by a military brigadier, those he returned to power ultimately hanged him for plotting a coup! The principle that largely won the sun party the general elections was rammed down our throats, and suddenly, in 1978, our country became a one-party state. Whatever hope of glory that remained was extinguished, and slowly but surely our country sank into a morass. In this new disturbing dawn, all had to toe the line, as we all flew the same flag. Even the greedy and self-seeking members of the opposition were jostling for positions, ministerial or otherwise, under the excuse that we were all under the same banner. This swing tendency, defined as "chameleonic" in the report of the Truth and Reconciliation Commission, is prevalent, particularly among politicians of our country. Thankfully, there was one man, a single-minded individual, now deceased, who stuck to his guns and ideology by never joining in the rat race. Even in the Chamber of Parliament, he would sit alone on the opposition side and be the lone voice of opposition. Now that our country is once again practicing democracy, those who exculpate themselves from the woeful and disastrous rule of that era should take note. Of course, they had a choice but were propelled by their greed and selfishness, and they used their thirst for power as a means of illegally enriching themselves.

As usual with regime change, expectations were high when the APC government was installed in the late sixties. Up to a point, soon after assuming office, the government did not disappoint. But this did not last for long, and down the road, the true colours of the regime started to emerge. During the period of campaign, Siaka Stevens, the party leader, publicly pronounced, *"You see soak lepet you call am puss."* (You see a wolf in sheep's clothing.) We all thought then that he was a witty fellow, though his docility was deceptive; he could rise and be firm. Little did we realize that he was a wolf in sheep's clothing.

Once he had received the baton of state leadership, he became a very popular leader as time progressed. He would theatrically express his desire to retire while the electorate would clamour for his stay. In his flip-flops, he also declared, *"Pass ah die,"* meaning he would remain president for life. As providence would have it, he was unable to keep that promise; in the end, his physical state overcame his will, and he had to give up power.

During his tenure of office, he perhaps set the paradigm for social and behavioural change by his pronouncements, which one might take as policy, seeing that such pronouncements were uttered by the head of state. He was not a metaphysical poet in a paradoxical jest. In fact, a head of state has no business jesting in such serious matters of state. During one of his public utterances in Krio, the lingua franca, he upended a national value by saying, *"Dem say Bailor Barrie; you say Davidson Nicol."* The import was this: contrary to traditional wisdom, Bailor Barrie is more important than Davidson Nicol. Davidson Nicol was an intellectual icon but not seen to be rich while Bailor Barrie was an illiterate businessman but very wealthy. Why then are we perplexed at the current state of our educational system?

What country in this global age cannot boast of even a single serious bookshop? Sad to say, in our country, the former "Athens of West Africa," there is not a single bookshop worth the name. Some old books are sold on the ground in *gron bookshops* (books placed on the ground for sale). In cases of sheer necessity, when certain books need to be made available, intellectual property rights are ground to non-existence by the impudence of all-day churning photocopiers. To publish is a punishable crime. In the same vein of his untamed theatricalities, Stevens also publicly pronounced, *"Nar sense make book nor to book make sense."* The interpretation is that it is better to be street-wise than school-wise. So why should we be ashamed of the rate of illiteracy prevailing in our country?

Being street-wise was a triumph over your environment. Well, in another interpretation, Stevens used his sense to write a book, the 1978 one-party constitution, but it turned out that that did not make sense. It reads like an unabashed, disgraceful hijacking of state governance by an unholy gang leader and his gang and had to be repealed and replaced by the 1991 democratic constitution during the Momoh regime. In sheep's clothing during a 1967 elections campaign at Brookfields National Stadium, Stevens had roused people to rave and cry to the starry sky with hope, with upraised fists punching the air, "Power belongs to the people! Power belongs to the people!" Clearly for him, that people's power was only useful and operable to lift him up to power riding on popular grievances such as the unacceptable tribalistic grip on the land by Albert Margai's SLPP regime.

Stevens treated Albert's degeneration to reckless and dangerous tribalism in his book *What Life Has Taught Me.* But he himself had his own form of nightmare waiting in the shadows, for the people in a one-party lockdown. This same leader, who led by example, further turned the ethical value of accountability on its head, publicly declaring, *"Oosie dem tie cow nar dae ee go eat grass."* Interpretation: make the most of any opportunity coming your way, by fair means or foul. Thus, those in high places had a field day. At some point in time, dipping into the treasury became the order of the day. It got so bad that any number of scams was initiated even by the lower ranks to fleece government coffers. When it got out of hand, the voucher-gate affair was unearthed and became a big scandal. Then the government was fleeced out of millions of leones. Cutting a long story short, most of those found wanting disappeared from public life temporarily, after which they resurfaced and were recycled into the system, in most cases into higher positions. Not surprisingly, another financial scandal was unearthed, this time described as "squander gate."

The latter period of the old man's regime was characterised by scarcity of rice, our staple food, petrol, and foreign exchange. Our country, with all its resources, has always been import dependent, more of a consumer than a production society. Imagine! Even with a central monetary authority, our central bank, the foreign exchange price was determined by one man, Jamil Sahid Mohamed, who was not a member of the government but could sit in Cabinet. As for rice, it became a political tool as it was bought not with money but with "chits" distributed by the old man himself to self-styled Hajas who knew almost next to nothing about rice other than their personal consumption. They were the ones determining the price of this scarce staple food and making super-normal profits on the heads of our poor countrymen.

Another national bane was the military's obsession with coups d'état. Apparently, the military in the West African region assessed themselves as being potentially more proficient in the luxuries of state governance than in their own hard and hazardous discipline. Perhaps they were simply jealous of civilian governments swimming in paradise, and pretending to run and develop a country, while they swam on dry ground in bush training, although they were practically safe from wars and actual opposing combatants. Or having tasted the sweet fruits of what they had in their own budget, they wanted to be in charge of the whole thing. From the inception of his election to power, Stevens was sorely plagued by the military. And this torment went down the line to Ahmed Tejan Kabbah's SLPP governments after Albert Margai of the SLPP first released the evil genie from the bottle in 1967. Now, we recall that in his book *What Life Has Taught Me*, Stevens attributes the decline of Albert's leadership resources to his adverse experiences. "The setbacks he had suffered had embittered, even corrupted him." For his own part, did he, from his own torment by the military decline, to the viewpoint that man is a beast and should be treated as such?

In that event, he should have taken the proper course, washed his hands off the so-called Athens of West Africa, and retired to the bush following the footsteps of Shakespeare's archetypal Timon of Athens. However, during his watch, to bring the errant security forces on board and in tune with his regime, and perhaps to stave off coups and counter-coups, he appointed the heads of the military and the police to Parliament. Strange bedfellows.

The national one-party constitution of 1978 provided that the vice president succeeds the president on his retirement. However, by the time the old man retired, he had mischievously tinkered with the constitution to prevent his second-in-command, who had been a loyal friend through thick and thin, and prominent in his politics of violence, from succeeding him. He chose instead a relative novice, the head of the army, at the time a sitting Member of Parliament. Conspiracy theories abounded why this choice. The preponderant hope, all the same, was that, he being a military asset, his personality would calm the restlessness of the military, since their man was now president and, so relieved, enjoy ample room to concentrate on turning around the national decline for life to become better. No matter what the conspiracy theorists propounded—notwithstanding the fanfare proclamation of a new order, the positing of the philosophy of constructive nationalism, his interesting, opening salvo on a control on foreign-exchange transactions, and a promised sufficiency in rice production to stop rice-importation through a return of migrants from the cities to the farms—our country continued to slide and the quality of life deteriorated. Unfortunately, the brigadier-general was not up to the task and had to publicly confess over the airwaves that he was a failure. But realizing that fact, did he take the honourable step of resigning? No, he had the temerity to continue as a failure, egged on by his ill-disciplined and unscrupulous cabal.

Now, in his book *The Agony of a Nation*, the proud foreign minister of this regime uncovers, from the inside, some of these failures: incredible bungling, apparent, recurrent loss of state funds to smooth international conmen, and brazen and reckless corruption, all at the ultimate, high core of state governance. But interestingly, he distances himself not only cleanly from the villainies around but also from both collective cabinet responsibility and his alternative obligation to resign.

Momoh not only did not resign or sack some of his ministers who may not have served him well, but he wanted another five-year term in office, having won the party leadership at the October 1991 convention of the one recognized party.

Now an irrational tragedy in Sierra Leone is that it has a number of square pegs in round holes who amazingly do not have the least bit awareness that they are square pegs. Or if they think that, they do not think it is untenable for them to sit in round holes. Perhaps they think that, after all, we are all square pegs all across the nation. One highly placed square peg falls on a lowly square peg and boots him out for incompetence, only for him to be later exposed as a square peg lounging in a round hole. Anyway, one has to be rock solid to dare to bring a square peg to the awareness that he is a square peg, for otherwise you should prepare to "die" one way or another.

Characteristically, Momoh failed to deliver when the country (to use the language of in memoriams) needed him most. Generally, Liberians respected Sierra Leoneans for their love of education and their pursuit of development in personal refinement. A mere corporal, Foday Sankoh, a photographer, and his band of the benighted humiliated our proud people under the heels of a Liberian Lilliputian, a vicious beast called Charles Taylor. Together they ravaged our land, slaughtering our people, terrorist style, in a manner not even the insane would think of slaughtering animals. What serious preparations did our leaders make, with all-important foresight, from Sir Milton to Joseph Saidu Momoh, in thirty years of nationhood (1961–1991) to meet such eventuality? A brigadier-general and former force-commander sitting as president of the republic and commander-in-chief of the armed forces, supported by Nigerian and Guinean troops, by the Chinese, the Americans, the British, could not rally, inspire, and command all his legion of comrades from major-general to lieutenants to privates summarily to end the carnage.

A window into the shock and dismay of Sierra Leoneans is their euphoria at a State House rally vis-à-vis the disillusioning events of the prosecution of the war. At a popular rally called by President Momoh at the forecourt of State House to explain the outbreak of rebel hostilities supported by Taylor's NPFL fighters, the people were certain Taylor had chewed off more than he could swallow. With our fine array of top military brass, reds and pips and crowns, our long tradition of proficient soldiering, the Sandhurst trained, Nigerian trained. Taylor and Sankoh had made the greatest mistake in their miserable lives in daring to annoy Sierra Leone. The people danced and sang in Krio, "Give me the ammunition. I want to go to the battlefield." And our response would not be simply to boot out the scum from our native land that we love, our Sierra Leone. We would penetrate deep into Liberia and destroy Taylor at his Gbarnga base. They raised their hands and raved and screamed, "All the way to Gbarnga! All the way to Gbarnga!" That was the army we thought we had. That was what we expected of Momoh, the right man in the right place at the right time. Not the funereal report of rebels picking up town after town after town, entrenching themselves. Our troops reported later "flushing them out," or driving them across the border, only for them to return and penetrate even deeper into our territory.

Ah, all was reactive after free, unchallenged rape and slaughter and abductions to swell their ranks and become deadlier, after looting to fund and feed their designs. Never once proactive to prevent them, never seizing the initiative to take the war to the enemy. Soldiers and civilians alike panicked and hotly fled at the fake sounds of heavy firepower. One could imagine Sankoh laughing and boosting the morale of his men. "I told you so. They are nothing really, just parade, parade, coups, coups." Actual, orderly, tactical retreat could have shortly uncovered the fake for the campaign to continue. All the same, by some calm, decisive plan sitting on seething patriotic rage, Sankoh and Taylor should have been made to rue the day and damn the hour they insulted our military. For the overriding common sense and constitutional function of our armed forces is to protect us with the arms they are provided with and trained to use.

Well, a war is not the colourful spectacle of a proud poppy day parade, a presidential guard of honour, a wistful beating of the retreat, or a military tattoo, where if ragtag, indecent rebels arrived to take part, they would be laughed to scorn. But we had thought that in our case, at least, all that ceremonial pomp and pageantry stood on and reflected a rock foundation of bravery and proficiency vastly superior to a rebel caricature of soldiering. Otherwise, no excuses. Common sense dictates that all or some of the soldiers are trained as guerrillas, if that is what works. At the first acid test of the robust continuity of Mahyoung by the inheritors, the great and revered names of our armed forces all foundered to the feet of dumbfounded national consternation, for the inception of a severe national trauma.

To his credit, however, Momoh promulgated the 1991 multiparty constitution, his legacy, which is being currently used. In spite of the group of his Limba tribesmen, Ekutay, that he had around him, which his power-hungry detractors dubbed his "Kitchen Cabinet" and vehemently accused him of tribalism, for one who has seen the ugly, dangerous face of tribalism, I think he was not, at least, a convincing tribalist. He would unite the country if he could. Now there was a minister who, when his scholarship committee presented for his approval its list of successful candidates for government bursaries, would curse foully, foam at the mouth like Wole Soyinka's president Kongi, and vigorously scratch out with his mighty pen the names he connected with a hated tribe. He would declare, "Now is our time; they had their time!"

Certainly, such a nefarious policy, riding on the back of government funds, is unacceptable. At least in their visible on-stage performances, neither President Siaka Stevens nor President Tejan Kabbah was a tribalist, which was a blessing. Momoh was more a man passionate about the good life, fun, and games, a man of wine, many pretty women, and Lagoonda (a pleasure complex on the banks of the Sierra Leone River, with which he is intimately associated in the public mind). He did try to do some good things. He could have suffered the fate of President Laurent Kabila, when he courageously sought to limit the ubiquitous power of the chief patron and financier of his presidential, electioneering campaign, the diamond magnate, power-drunk Jamil Sahid Mohamed, whom Siaka Stevens had made a virtual "co-president" of Sierra Leone, dishonouring his country. Momoh tried to take Jamil's hands off the presidency, concentrate them on business, and the "co-president" did not like it.

Now, following his stern warning against election violence in 1991, he acted swiftly and solitarily against one of his own close supporters and tribesman, disqualifying him from the race to send an unmistakable message that he meant what he said. This was a shock funeral among his tribesmen—irreversible death.

Hitherto, election violence was the diabolical hallmark of our rigged elections. To the unenlightened and even the apparently enlightened, the return of many unopposed candidates through overt violence at elections was like a glorious, proud invention made in Sierra Leone. One of the vice presidents of the APC and chief architect of violence was popularly referred to as *"Agba Satanie"* (Boss Satan). He was said to have boasted that he had ninety-nine ways to win an election and that the only thing a government in power could not do was to change a man into a woman and vice-versa. (That of course, was before the known technology of sex change.) In a word, the figurative phrase *fight for power* was very literally enacted by chiefs, drugged thugs, and other supporters everywhere. Not many women dared to enter such a war for unsafe seats. But Momoh was sorely tormented by various threats to overthrow his government. "Uneasy lies the head that wears the golden crown." This should have been comparative child's play for a former force commander who could have been called upon to defend his land against foreign aggression. However, fearing the growing intrigue around him, especially when he finally dropped many of his ministers to face another election in 1991, relying on the genuine support of his own tribesmen, he allowed the inspector-general of police, Bambay Kamara, of his Limba tribe, to upset his little virtues and use strong-arm methods against those he perceived as enemies to the president's success.

All the foregoing, failed leadership, pervasive corruption among the elite class, absence of redress in the legal and justice system, and of course, inequitable distribution of wealth constitute the context of the rebel war. But were they the actual main cause of Foday Sankoh's war?

"By their fruits ye shall know them." Obvious to actual empirical observation, the rebel war was nasty, unjust, and ignoble. It revealed the mind of Sankoh and his rebels. The delineated context of the war could have been the cause of a noble and just war. But the rebel war was not a noble and just war, so the authentic context of the war was not as The Truth and Reconciliation Commission Report makes it the cause of the war. Or if we like, it was not the dominant cause of Sankoh's war.

Of course, the report is excellent and very readable. The historical antecedents to the war are brilliantly captured and documented. So also is the work on the nature of the war. But as if mechanically following models or theories, there is a worrying contradiction and disconnect in the TRC report between what is held up as the cause of the war and the diabolical war itself. We correct this distorted line for a symbiotic cause and effect when we posit the unbridled lust for political power, the will to swim in state luxuries without serious intentions, and commitment as the dominant cause of the war. It was a continuation, grotesquely amplified into a senseless insurrection, of the masked intentions of politicians and coupists alike all down the line to Sankoh. There was not even a single patriotic Brutus in the rebel ranks of Corporal Foday Sankoh. This should be emphasized, even for present thinking on the war, and especially for posterity that will be far removed from the experience of it.

CHAPTER 2

MAY DAY, DARKNESS AT DAWN

House on fire.

Rag-tag rebel group

Indeed, 25 May 1997 heralded a special and singular epoch in the political history of Sierra Leone. Never before had a singular incident which turned into an event triggered such a response from the world at large. The military takeover was roundly and unequivocally condemned by the world populace, and rightly so. Less than a year after constitutional democratic rule was established, after passably free and fair presidential and parliamentary elections, the armed forces, who for several years were fighting against rebel insurgents, to the dismay and disbelief of Sierra Leoneans, joined forces with their arch and supposedly bitter foe to abrogate the democratic rights of all peace loving Sierra Leoneans. Their excuse? They were bringing peace to a country devastated by several years of civil strife through the AFRC-RUF junta and the People's Army.

For years, the taxpayers were contributing their hard-earned income to support our disappointing soldiers, only for them to turn their guns upon the innocent population, thus vindicating the suspicion that these soldiers were *sobels* (soldiers turned rebels). They had vociferously contested this suspicion, which an enquiry sought to investigate. But now the soldiers had brought "peace" to our strife-ridden country through abominable treachery; the rebels, who were in the bush for so long, were now occupying the seat of power, commandeering houses from city dwellers who had spent their lives serving the nation diligently, and all their sweat from toil and travail to build those houses. This dastardly act was perpetrated in localities in the capital and its environs. And it did not stop there. The best hotels in the city became a haven for the rebels. True to form, after commandeering these hotels, they ultimately pillaged and vandalized them. Being used to living in the jungle, all they knew about the finer things in life was to sleep on the floor (a laudable act) and use the hotel furniture as firewood for cooking. It then became blurring whether Johnny Paul Koroma and his group of ragamuffins were tourists on a temporary sojourn to enjoy the nice things and spots in the country or indeed were serious in holding the reins of power. Even after nine months, they still could not make up their minds. Unfortunately, Sierra Leoneans continued to suffer because of sobel intransigence and bestial acts.

Why should they vacate their unholy seat of power occupied by force of arms, the very same they used to enforce the peace they claimed to have brought to the country? With their coming, political theory was to be rewritten. They had given new interpretation to democracy, the rule of law, human rights, and so on. For them, the ballot box was an anachronism, democracy could only be established through the barrel of the gun, and everybody would fall in line. How they miscalculated! The so-called peace they brought meant silencing the will of the majority and abhorring dissent. How paradoxical that when they seized power, they gave as one of their excuses promoting the freedom of the press, thinking that they would win the support of the press, as press freedom had always been a thorny issue under successive regimes. However, when the press failed to fall in line, they were muzzled and locked up in windowless containers, which apparently became the final resting place of those who did not see eye to eye with the junta forces.

Dissent was not to be tolerated; perhaps, under their definition of democracy, it was a crime to be put down violently. They were also very partial in their policies and actions. How could one explain the discriminatory application of their laws in regulating our society? Take the act of demonstrations. The sobels unashamedly allowed their often drugged and paid sympathizers to march in support of their regime but prevented other groups from showing their contempt and disregard, which were legitimate, considering the way and manner the junta assumed power. The students' protest called for months after the coup was violently quelled. Never before did our citizenry witness such acts of cruelty and callous abandon. Then the true character of the rebel movement was further unveiled. Not only did they go after the students and those identified as students, slaughtering and maiming, because of their mode of dress or looks, with heavy weaponry—anti-aircraft guns, machine guns, etc.—but they also had their stock in trade, machetes, which were looted from stocks that had been stored for the rehabilitation and reconstruction of the very country they had devastated. These machetes were part of a package that had been assembled for rehabilitating farms in the most productive areas affected by the rebel war. These misfits thought that reducing the population by slaughtering was a more efficient solution to our food security problem than increasing food production.

**Rebel fighter posing with AK 47 rifle and
Rocket Propelled Grenade (RPG)**

Even the hospitals did not prove a place of refuge, as some students who had been admitted to hospitals were attacked. Not surprisingly, if a church or mosque was not sacrosanct, how could a hospital be sacrosanct? On the day of the coup, some churches were vandalized and looted a black day in which the doors of many of our churches were closed. In truth, this had never happened before in our nation's short history. It did not stop there. The doors of our churches also remained closed some weeks after the coup when the sobels again decided to mount a demonstration against ECOMOG troops at Jui. Then it was decided that those who went to church, as it was on a Sunday, would be used as human shields. They were going to be shepherded against their will, like sheep by the AFRC-RUF strong-arm thugs, to be used as cannon fodder to satisfy their animal bestiality. As news of this strategy filtered through church corridors, church leaders advised their various congregations to stay away.

Succinctly, selecting at random to convey through image only a peep into AFRC-RUF insanity and the terror that entrapped a defenceless population—the Holy Trinity Church at Kissy Road was torched and had to be very extensively rehabilitated. Also torched was the Truscott Church at Kissy Road; it has been rebuilt. The Big Market at Wallace Johnson Street, a traditional monument where generations of lowly grassroots traders, mainly women, sold traditional, native, and West African items to eke out their means of livelihood, was set on fire and had to be rebuilt. The Ministry of Finance, a very sturdy colonial structure, was set ablaze and has been extensively rehabilitated. Wonder upon wonders! Even a section of the central bank was torched.

Happenings in our country have been an eye opener, at the end of which it is hoped that it will be a better country. Will it? Won't we be up to our old tricks of politicking and sycophantic behaviour, kowtowing to ministers, singing the praises of those in authority, knowing they are performing badly, glorifying those who rape public coffers as long as a treacle of these ill-gotten gains trickle down? And, very upsetting, much of the vicious criticisms of the detractors of those in power are launched by people who are themselves no better in any shape or form than their targets. They have only selfish eyes on the prize of power—not to be held in trust for the entire nation, for development and fair distribution of national wealth—but for self and, predominantly, tribe. We also cannot romanticize the people; some of them are clearly evil, very selfish, unjust, and murderous. With lies, some manipulated relatives, friends, and acquaintances in the rampaging forces to execute their personal vendetta: destruction and death for petty jealousies and for even spurned invitations to infidelity.

The repercussions of this act of lunacy perpetrated by the military and rebel elements reverberated far and wide. Months after the coup, the junta had yet to consolidate its authority. Interestingly enough, they vociferously proclaimed they were the government. In their confused and simple minds, they failed to understand the intricacies of politics and international relations, not to talk of economics and finance. Witness in 1992 when the NPRC seized power in a previous military takeover of a corrupt and paralysed government. Within a month, they became the de facto government as they were acclaimed by the people of Sierra Leone and also recognized by the international community, and business went on as usual.

With the AFRIC-RUF, the situation was different. It was apparent that their might—acquired through their weapons—had placed them in authority over a deceptively tame but resilient people who, armed with only their determination and courage, resisted the might and bestiality of the rebels, refusing to be subjugated by force of arms alone. Intelligence and cajolery may have succeeded where the gun had failed. Alas, the actions of the junta boys illustrated their deficiencies in this area. In short, although they were deluded into believing their primacy in government, they were not the de facto government. If they had succeeded in that, our country would have become a failed state long before the new millennium. Even within this short time, the country was moribund.

Johnny Paul Koroma had a vision for the beginning of the millennium, namely death of a nation. What a fitting epitaph it would have been! Being a very religious but unrighteous soul, he was misconstruing Armageddon for the demise of our country, not even the end of this global civilization. He was not alone. The world is full of apocalyptic people who relate the end of the twentieth century to the cataclysmic end of the present age.

Had they been right in their prediction, according to biblical prophecy, the acts of Johnny Paul Koroma and his comrades-in-arms would have depicted "signs of the end time." However, if that had been the case, they would not have escaped the scourge of the "beast." Johnny Paul Koroma proclaimed himself to be religious, but piety was not one of his attributes, and as a result, the country suffered. Perhaps he was more of a professing Christian than a practising one. One may enquire though what religion had to do with it. "Nothing" would be the reply, but for the fact that we in our country have more often than not likened ourselves to the biblical children of Israel. And as was pinpointed earlier on, the very same Johnny Paul Koroma pledged not his services but the nation to the Almighty. If we were superstitious, we might have attributed our woes to the scourge of the Almighty because of his mockery and mock religiosity.

Now, both the people of the Land of the Free and the entire international world order totally rejected the AFRC-RUF junta. This was amply demonstrated by the civil disobedience of the nation and the complete isolation of the junta by the international community. They were roundly and soundly condemned by the Organisation of African Unity (the OAU), the Economic Community of West African States (ECOWAS), the European Union (EU), and the United Nations (UN). As a result, all the international donor agencies, the entire diplomatic corps, and bilateral aid organizations left and ceased to do business with our country. In their determination to rid the world, especially the continent of Africa, of military dictatorship, they eschewed vehemently doing business with the junta. Since the junta was left to themselves and they were the de facto government, they still maintained a foreign affairs ministry with full staff complement and a secretary of state for foreign affairs. Paradoxically, they downgraded the reconstruction ministry to a commission, but did they have the staff and resources to run it, let alone maintain a semblance of reconstruction?

The sobels surely knew how to destroy but not how to rebuild. They should not have assumed that because Liberia chose Charles Taylor as president in order to spearhead the rebuilding of Liberia since, among others, he was responsible for its wrecking, therefore as of right, this should be replicated in our country. If they understood the mechanics of development, structural adjustment, reconstruction, and rehabilitation, they would not have alienated the entire donor community.

Over 90 per cent of investment flows had been sourced from bilateral and multilateral sources. It was rather unfortunate that at the time of the coup, Sierra Leone was at the point of takeoff. Government, in this case the de jure Kabbah government, had concluded negotiations with the World Bank and the International Monetary Fund for another phase of the structural adjustment and the reconstruction and rehabilitation programmes, including a safety net programme for the youth and other vulnerable groups. The European Union had already incepted a reconstruction programme in some parts of the provinces. The World Bank had already approved twenty-seven projects costing nearly one billion leones as pilot programme which was to start almost immediately. The Islamic Development Bank also had lodged two million dollars with the central bank as a contribution to the government's rehabilitation effort. As the events that ushered in the darkness of 25 May 1997 appeared unbelievable to many countrymen, so did the wanton destruction of both life and property that followed seem beyond comprehension, hence the adverse reactions of nationals and foreigners to junta rule.

CHAPTER 3

DESCENT INTO HELL

Burnt Out Village

The sobels were neither discriminatory nor selective in their actions to ravage the city of Freetown, its inhabitants, historical monuments, the diplomatic corps and their assets, government buildings, petty traders, the old and infirm, hospitals, nursing homes and clinics, schools and colleges, etc. Nothing and no one escaped the wrath of our so-called "liberators." Surprisingly, they thought prisoners, even those condemned for murder, were being "oppressed," so they all had to be liberated. And then to aggravate an already deplorable situation, they were all given AK-47 automatic rifles and uniforms to continue the liberation struggle. In his maiden speech, Corporal Tamba Gborie said that all the inputs were in place.

To this day, we have not been able to fathom or decipher the contents of that maiden speech. Perhaps it was so nonsensical even to the ears of the coup makers that the next set of speeches had to be made by a different spokesman. Note that in April 1992, when the Khaki Boys mistakingly staged their coup, a major gave the initial broadcast, but soon after, Captain Strasser, who was to become the chairman, went on the air. With the sobels' coup, the situation was different. The man who was to be chairman was languishing in jail. So the initial broadcast to the nation was long in coming. Unfortunately, even the so-called second in command, the vice chairman could not make the broadcast then as he himself was languishing under house arrest in a foreign country, for committing a criminal offence. What a travesty that the leader and vice leader of a country with such heritage and promise were jailbirds—jailed not for being prisoners of conscience but for criminal offences. (If one was to examine closely the cultural and social dynamics of the rebel movement, one would not be surprised at the 25 May incident and subsequent events.)

A topical question to which many of us Sierra Leoneans will not be privy to the answer is this: Who staged the coup? Was it the military, the rebels, or the sobels? The soldiers led us to believe that it was a military putsch and not a rebel takeover of the government. The putsch happened on a Sunday. By Monday, the soldiers made a broadcast inviting the rebels to join this circus, and by the following day, Tuesday, the capital city was awash with rebel elements turbaned in red headband and diabolically bloody. How could this have happened when, according to newspaper reports and editorials, the rebel movement as a military force was almost a spent force, its members malnourished and ill equipped? Where did they suddenly spring from, and with so much weaponry? Something was definitely very wrong in the going-on in our country.

But that was not all. Rumours of coup plots had been circulating all over the country; some were reported in the daily newspapers, but were they taken seriously? Even our seemingly revered head of state and command-er-in-chief of the armed forces made a statement indicating his knowledge of the planned coup some three days before the event. However, it would appear nothing was done, but one should not have forgotten that he was a man of peace. Because of this inaction on the part of the head of state, our country became a real jungle for ten months in the short run and many more years in the long term. If he took any action unbeknown to the public, they were grossly inadequate, as subsequent events proved. If one was superstitious, it would have been difficult to not have believed that this was in the cards. No matter how inept or corrupt the government of the day was, the forceful overthrow of a legitimate government did not bode well for our fledgling democracy.

Evidently, to all and sundry alike, the so-called solution taken by the military did result in a worse situation. During their reign of terror, the country was plunged into the abyss by their acts of intimidation, murder, commandeering of private and public assets, and a general state of may-hem. Unfortunately, they had neither the intelligence nor the vision to have foreseen the path to which they were taking the country. By our reckoning, we did regress about fifty years. In simple terms, that is a half-century, longer than the average lifespan of countrymen. In essence, many of our present generation will not live long enough to see our beloved country achieve its place in the global community. Coming closer to home, many of us would have to struggle to put our country back on its feet without having the pleasure of reaping the rewards of our labours.

Since it is easier to destroy than to build or create, it will take generations to put our country on its aching feet, especially with the lackadaisical attitude of officialdom. There are many facets of the country to be reconstructed and rehabilitated: the economy; our financial institutions, including the treasury, burnt down by the sobels as their own method of ridding the country of corruption; our physical infrastructure; our health and educational system; family life; and other relationships. The entire fabric of our society was turned upside down. It all seemed so confusing, considering that the country was undergoing structural adjustment, trying to come to terms with a decade of economic mismanagement, endemic corruption, and the after-effects of a senseless war. Ironically, only Sankoh, who was languishing in jail in foreign territory, and perhaps Charles Taylor, his benefactor, were deluded into believing they were fighting for a just cause where the means never justified the ends in this case. It was one of the sobel spokesmen in an interview over the BBC in a Focus on Africa Programme who admitted that the rebel war in our country was senseless. Yet these very same boys, by inference, risked their necks to topple a legitimately elected government because of this "senseless" war that the rebels in cahoots with the military were pursuing.

Collection of heads of beheaded victims.

Alas! What a calamity that befell our country. People might say it was the scourge of the Devil himself. Try as one might, it was very difficult to rationalise the actions of the military. Were they so weak that they had to invite the Devil to assist them in their untimely and foolish actions to maintain and prop up their unpopular military regime? Indeed, in their quest for recognition, they did try to win the sympathy of the Ghanaian president who was himself an experienced military coup implementer (he staged two successful military coups in Ghana), only to be castigated for joining with rebels to stage a coup. How could an army have indulged in such machinations if it were professional and disciplined? As it turned out, for all was revealed, billions of Leones of taxpayers' money were squandered by the military top brass. This being so, the foot soldiers found their own ways of profiting from the war by joining the rebels to pillage, loot, and rape innocent citizens. At the height of the conflict, all this was conjecture, but as events on and after 25 May unfolded, our greatest fears were realised. Our soldiers were no longer on our side but on the side of greed and self-aggrandisement.

Imagine the army, which is supposed to be the last bastion of discipline and integrity, was corrupt. This should, however, not come as a surprise. A corrupt regime, led by Momoh, the president, at the start of the war, disregarded all the rules of a disciplined army by recruiting robbers, vandals, dropouts, and drug addicts beneath the motto "Come one, come all. Seats free. No collection." Similarly, at the height of the rebel incursion after the soldiers under the nickname "Khaki boys" came into power in 1992, they themselves instituted a massive recruitment drive in aid of fighting the rebels who were making inroads in the south and north of the country. Curiously, the qualification for recruitment was to be able to haul a nine-foot by nine-foot concrete block from Congo Cross in the Western side of the Freetown to the famous Cotton Tree at the central part of the city, a distance of between two and three kilometres. Again, as in previous occasions, many dropouts and good-for-nothings found their way into the national army. Due to the pressing state of the war which was then raging in the diamondiferous and agriculturally productive areas, these relatively untried and untested would-be soldiers were put through three months of training before being thrown into the cauldron. Among incompetence, greed, corruption, and collusion, is it any wonder that the conflict dragged on and on, finally ending after just over a decade?

To pacify the sobels, a peace conference was organised by the international community to discuss the challenge of peace before or after a general election. The people were adamant and unequivocally registered their discontent at the military, emphatically stating their choice for elections and a return to a democratic government. Against their will (they had very little choice), the Khaki Boys, after five years in power, decided to relinquish the reins of government to a legitimately elected government, a process which was duly effected in March 1996 after a general election (some people thought was rigged) that pitchforked the Palm Tree Party, led by the international Tejan Kabbah, into government. By April of the same year, a democratically elected government was installed in the country, after twenty-five years of one-party mismanagement and five years of military dictatorship.

Within a year of taking office, the government, led by Tejan Kabbah, succeeded in signing a peace accord with the rebel movement led by who else? Sankoh. Unfortunately, most of the provisions of the accord reached on that fateful November day in 1996 had not been implemented (by the time of the sobels' military coup), mainly due to the intransigence of the rebel leader. Also, by the time of the coup, the rebel movement was split. To the utter dismay of many of us, the SLPP government publicly recognised and undiplomatically dealt with a splinter faction while trying against all odds to implement the peace accord. How ill advised that action was! How could a government consisting of experts in diplomacy commit such a blunder?

One immediate repercussion of that single act was the kidnapping and incarceration of the so-called leaders of the splinter faction and a member of the government's negotiating team. The sobels were claiming that the three leaders of the splinter group were still alive, but knowledge of rebel operation and behaviour would make us believe that they had been eliminated. The government member who was later released attested to their continued existence, but they have not been seen since. Foday Sankoh, the leader of the rebel movement, was a mad tyrant who brooked no dissent or opposition. Stories abound about his bloodthirstiness and voracious appetite for human suffering. To think that his so-called backers, notably Charles Taylor, who was the president of Liberia, championed his stake in our beloved country's political process! Surely, neither by merit nor by popular acclaim, did Corporal Sankoh deserve a stake in the political hegemony of Sierra Leone. Let no one draw a parallel with our neighbours. Taylor was perhaps fortunate (for a time) to be given the opportunity to rebuild the country that he and his comrades in arms destroyed. We Sierra

Leoneans are cast in a different mould. Even if an election was manipulated, Sankoh would not have won, albeit a moot point as he has been called to give account of his stewardship. Fortunately, our neighbours did not qualify to vote in our country. Above all else, he was a mass murderer and should have been treated as such; he and his colleagues should have been arraigned before a war crimes tribunal, like the one in The Hague before which Milosevic, former president of Yugoslavia, was arraigned. No matter what the stakes were, a negotiated settlement with the sobels was anathema to the majority of sane-thinking and peace-loving Sierra Leoneans. Sankoh and his foot soldiers, those who joined willingly and those who were conscripted like schoolchildren aged nine years and above, were the active players. What about the passive players, those whose real sympathies came to light after the military takeover?

It must have come as a shock when, a few days after the coup, no less a person than Dr John Karefa-Smart, a one-time political heavyweight, went on the radio to broadcast to the entire nation that he had intercepted a message concerning the bombardment of the capital city by ECOMOG forces to catapult the junta out of power. The operation, according to him, was code-named "Operation Wild Geese." At that time, it would appear he was passionately on the side of peace and freedom but against injustice and oppression. But lo and behold, as the drama unfolded, it became clear that a man of such stature, who had presidential aspirations and seemed to have believed in the democratic process, had an agenda of his own which was definitely not in tune with the democratic aspirations of peace-loving Sierra Leoneans. As it turned out, Karefa-Smart was not the only one to have championed the cause (whatever cause there was) of the sobels, in those early days, on the pretext of bringing peace to the country, no matter at what price. It turned out that Dr Abbas Bundu, another presidential hopeful, was pro-military and anti-democracy. These two political stalwarts, whether through hatred for the government or president or because of unbounded ambition and sour grapes, went all out *to rubbish* the country's strides towards the democratisation process. They advocated for the return to military dictatorship under the misguided belief that it would bring peace and stability to our country. Karefa-Smart and Abbas Bundu even went to great lengths to perjure the recently held elections and some of the ECOWAS accord. For what purpose? Were these gentlemen so power-hungry and thoughtless to even sacrifice the wishes of an entire nation just for their personal gain? They must have been as confused as the dropouts and drug addicts of the military junta. Strangely enough, after perpetrating their acts of infamy and failing, as was expected, they fled the country. They never had the guts or the decency to remain and tolerate *this glorious golden age* brought about by the military junta.

These two so-called political stalwarts were the champions of the sobels. Dr Abbas Bundu sent letters to the United Nations that were not even acknowledged, explaining the dangers of the so-called bombardment of Freetown by ECOMOG forces. What a disgrace for the chameleon, himself apparently a "seasoned diplomat," to be petitioning the UN Security Council as a private individual. A man with his intelligence should have realised that the democratic process had come to Sierra Leone and the people were fed up with military adventurism. Was he so selfish that he failed to sense the mood of the people at the Bintumani II peace conference? The elections were come and gone. He contested the elections and lost. Nevertheless, by virtue of his experience, he should have contributed to a paradigmatic change in governance and economic development.

Dr John Karefa-Smart, the octogenarian, indeed behaved in a similar manner. In some quarters, he was thought of as being senile. Not only was he sent on a mission abroad by the junta to mobilise support for military dictatorship, he even gave a press conference in New York at which he tied himself in knots. Poor man. Who was to blame? At his age, he should have retired gracefully to enjoy the fruits of his labours. He might have been up there once, in his youth perhaps, even at some period of his old age, but circumstances after the coup proved that he was past it.

As the junta rule stretched into months, their kith and kin and others of the same ilk jumped on the bandwagon. The Victor Fohs, Johnny Paul Koromas, Victor Brandons, Osho Williamses, Terrence Terries, Dr Johnsons, Hilton Fyles, and many others perhaps saw a chance for their names to be written down in history, no matter how ignominious. Fancy a junta who parlayed that they wanted to stamp out nepotism as one of their first acts and appointed the brother of JPK the chief of defence staff. Wonder of wonders, they were against tribalism, but the key players in this tragedy came from a very small tribe which happened to hail from the north of the country. Stranger still, on closer examination, their avid supporters and champions were members of the All People's Congress Party, which for twenty-five years led the country to ruination and decay.

As if this was not enough, the former president who fled the country after the 1992 coup returned to lend his support to the junta. All this followed after the current substantive holder had not only welcomed him back to his country but had also proposed an overly generous retirement package for him. As a show of gratitude, he stabbed him in the back. Perhaps he did this not as an ungrateful act but as an act of defiance and revenge against a nation which he misruled for over five years, draining most of the country's wealth, and which was livid with rage at the benefit package that had been put together for him. In a country where over 80 per cent of the people were considered poor, Joseph Saidu Momoh as an individual did not deserve those perks. After all, he was a failure; he said so himself. He was going to reap where and what he never planted.

Also, some people who were never in the mainstream of government, perhaps misguidedly, gave their unstilting support to the junta. These were the youths who thought they had been disadvantaged by the system, mainly school dropouts and semi-illiterate unemployed or underemployed. Many of them could not find gainful employment in the formal sector, because they lacked the necessary skills. However, rather than putting their effort into small-scale productive businesses, as opportunities abound in the informal sector, or learning some artisanal skills, they preferred roaming the streets of the capital, begging and/or engaging in pickpocketing and pilfering. Not surprisingly, the junta appealed to them; they were of the same family. In the early days of junta rule, Johnny Paul Koroma would pay them frequent visits at the Kroo Bay and their other popular sites. He must have felt comfortable with them. Hence, he would use those opportunities to make policy statements. It seemed as if they were his advisers. This was evidenced by some of the policy statements made and the manner in which they were delivered. Take for example Johnny Paul's vision statement. While the sobels had sent a delegation to the Ivory Coast to negotiate the peaceful handing over to the elected government, in the midst of it all, Johnny Paul Koroma delivered his vision statement to the nation without waiting for the response of the Ivorian government.

Talking about political gaffs, the sobels' track record was full of them. Were they really serious? Shortly after the coup, there were intense negotiations between the junta, on one side, and eminent personalities and the diplomatic corps on the other. As the story went, they had reached agreement on almost all the points (about twenty-one of them) raised by the junta. The next thing we knew, Johnny Paul Koroma went over the radio to broadcast the appointments of members to the ruling council, over forty of them. From that time onwards, Sierra Leoneans became suspicious of their intentions but not their sincerity, as events previously had proved that they were not honourable men. After the Johnny Paul Koroma vision speech fiasco, when he tried to explain that his vision 2001 was only an intention and not a statement of policy, they were given another chance to vacate the seat of government that they were usurping. Instead, they behaved like chameleons. After the first meeting, the sobels and the ECOWAS issued a communiqué on the handing over of the reins of government to the democratically elected government. To the consternation of Sierra Leoneans, and indeed the ECOWAS community, on the delegation's return to the city, a group which comprised, among others, of no less personalities than the octogenarian and Dr Abbas Bundu, a press conference was held, by which time the communiqué had been given a different meaning. The clause "to hand over power to the democratically elected government of President Ahmad Tejan Kabbah" was completely expunged from the joint communiqué.

As far as they were concerned, Tejan Kabbah was not an issue. And this became a topic of heated debate across the country. This also brought about the jumping into the sobels' bandwagon of those who never had the opportunity before to make their voices heard. Before then, the situation was very fluid. These sympathisers were unsure of the direction the wind was blowing. Apart from being greedy and corrupt, they were also opportunists and cowards who did not have any scruples or principles. This was the time Victor Foh chose to join the fray, and of course, he received his reward. The news was that he had been appointed chairman of telecommunications. Also rewarded was Dr Wiltshire Johnson (now deceased), who was appointed chairman of the Freetown City Council. He was only the chairman and not the mayor.

While our military had betrayed us, some who were thought to be eminent in their respective fields had let us down. Under normal circumstances, some of these individuals, would have been considered as being part of the elite, assuming there was still an elite class in Sierra Leone. As private individuals, they may have had grudges to pick with the establishment for seemingly past wrongdoings, but was this the way to seek redress? Educated they may have been, but was it possible that they were apparently unenlightened? Or was it just plain naiveté on their part that had led them not only to have supported but to have worked with this evil force?

It was very difficult to contemplate their actions; one could not have been so selfish and greedy as to have sold an entire nation to the Devil. One could only have concluded that they had no imagination. Without imagination, how would they have carried out and sustained this ***"one-stone" revolution?*** Apparently, they had plenty of dope to smoke in their respective offices to give them a high. Considering the complete isolation, both within and without that was confronting them, what business could they really have been carrying out in the offices? Amazing occurrences really.

After a five-year period of military rule, who would have thought the democratic process was only a short interlude heralding another spell of the boys in combat uniform. It never occurred to many of us Sierra Leoneans that we were only flirting with democracy. If we allowed him, Johnny Paul Koroma wanted to carry on until 2001, after which he would have ushered his own type of democracy, likely with Corporal Sankoh as the president of the First People's Republic. If that had happened, then Charles Taylor (as the president of Liberia) would have seen his dream fulfilled. One wondered then if he would have put his grand design into operation by annexing our country. Far-fetched? However, let us be optimistic. History has a way of repeating itself. In 1967, after a reasonable period of two-party rule, the military seized power but stayed for just over a year. After the military junta of the National Reformation Council was overthrown in 1968, civilian rule was restored, and under the All People's Congress Party, mismanagement and pillage dragged on for twenty-five years. This time round when the junta was ousted, it was our hope that we would have a long period of democratic good governance.

Unlike previous events in our country when only segments of society were affected, the events of the twenty-fifth of May and the following days affected all and sundry alike, all segments of society—indeed the entire country. During the years of civil strife which started in March 1991, many people were internally displaced while some others fled to neighbouring countries. After 25 May, a mass exodus of people took place from our country. People fled from Freetown and other provincial towns to neighbouring countries, and other countries as far away as the United States. The events of the coup were so traumatic that many people fled the country without having the opportunity to think about ways and means of sustaining their livelihood in foreign lands. On the other hand, many of our countrymen, those who left and those who stayed behind, thought that it would not have lasted beyond a few weeks, especially considering the sound condemnation it received from the international community: the OAU, the ECOWAS, the EU, and the United Nations.

While this was a period of great tribulation for many, for others, it was one of opportunity as they reaped super-normal gains out of the misery of the masses, as is usually the case worldwide in times of economic deprivation and war. Because of scarcity, in all branches of the economic system, the black economy flourished. It was a time when the official economic system was at either a standstill or regressing. It was even doubtful whether the country's economy generated any productive income during the entire reign of the sobel junta. The junta was even so cash-strapped that they could not even afford to pay themselves. But all things considered, they did not deserve payment for the terrible havoc they wreaked on lives and property.

So what was the policy, and how did the junta survive? As strange and incredible as it may sound, the junta leaders instructed their footmen, the soldiers, to pay themselves by looting the property of civilians. This policy was aptly named "Operation Pay Yourselves." Even the leaders were involved in what was a terrible time for Sierra Leoneans when looting was officially sanctioned by those leaders who were apparently the government of the day. It was rather unfortunate to learn from the radio news of theft of property by high-ranking sobel officials, and an order or appeal that the said stolen property be returned to its rightful owner. Many a time, the actions of these, our so-called leaders, shamed us. Robbery from innocent civilians was not their only speciality and not the only thing that many of us Sierra Leoneans were ashamed of. This military-rebel cabal was so bloodthirsty, and ruthless, that they did not hesitate to turn their guns on countrymen, killing and maiming men, women, and children just for propaganda against the ECOMOG forces. Many of us were aghast and left shell-shocked when on a fateful night there was much artillery fire and bombardment in the capital, which according to the junta left fifty innocent civilians dead. During that terrible night, the sobels were firing heavy artillery from strategic points in the city—Tower Hill, Fourah Bay College, and Falcon Bridge—deliberately into populated areas in the east end of town. This was not a figment of the imagination, as many people saw them perpetrating their evil acts. Some of them were even seen off-loading rocket propel grenades (RPGs) from Pajero and Mercedes-Benz cars, firing them at different points from Fourah Bay road in the east end of the city.

After this act of calumny, on the following day, the junta was vociferous in their propaganda against the ECOMOG forces, especially against Nigeria, claiming that their forces based at Lungi had shelled civilian habitations in the city, killing fifty people. In the quest of whipping up the people's wrath against Nigeria, the junta went ahead to desecrate the bodies of the victims by parading them around the streets in the centre of the capital to be finally laid at the doorsteps of the United Nations building, UN House. To complete this tragic farce, those who were supposedly the victims of the ECOMOG bombardment were given a mass burial service at the National Stadium, with Chairman Johnny Paul himself leading the service. Strangely, fifty people were reported killed, but there were only eighteen coffins. Rumour had it that some coffins contained more than one corpse. For Johnny Paul and his cabal, they might have thought this was a propaganda coup, but for many of us sensible Sierra Leoneans and the world community, this was an abhorrent act. We were embarrassed because of the shameful way the junta wanted to be accepted, stopping at nothing to gain popular acceptance by this stratagem.

As the mass exodus of Sierra Leoneans did not abate after the coup, many people were of the opinion that apart from the actions of the coup makers, the threat of ECOMOG bombardment aggravated the temporary shifting of the population. This was a propaganda that was vigorously pursued by the junta in trying to gain sympathy but failing woefully as their propaganda was so transparent, and their actions towards the populace contrary and irrational. It was inconceivable that such an oppressive regime wanted acclamation from the people they had put under the yoke. Nobody in his or her right mind could have supported them. But support they did receive from people of the same ilk, drawn from various groups: politicians, lawyers, doctors, etc.—people who, it turned out, were mere opportunists and limelight seekers. Certainly, they were not people of integrity.

It was disgraceful for a so-called mayor not to know the boundaries of his municipality. Many of us, countrymen, were astounded on hearing an interview over the BBC during which the sobel-appointed mayor of Freetown, Wiltshire Johnson, described the city as being bounded on the west by Juba and on the east by Allen Town. In their ignorance, that was perhaps the new conurbation by the junta. Perhaps Wiltshire should be excused. He was only partially to be blamed for his ignorance. Since the days of Siaka Probyn Stevens and his APC Party, they had done away with municipal elections. For a long time, the city had not enjoyed municipal elections but the APC fabricated a system in which councillors and chairperson were appointed and not elected by the people. We had them all throughout the days of the APC and one-party rule. With all this carnage and abuse of human dignity, it was not surprising that many Sierra Leoneans left the country under uncertain and fluid conditions.

At the onset of the conflict, there were the fortunate ones who were evacuated by the British, the French, and the Americans. The British, French, and Americans were evacuating their nationals from a country that had become lawless, ungovernable, and inhospitable even to its own nationals. During the evacuation exercise, the scene at the Mammy Yoko and Cape Sierra Hotels at the western side of the city's Peninsular was quite chaotic, tense, and pathetic. The situation was so desperate that many people who were not nationals of these countries, both old and young, packed their meagre possessions, waiting to be evacuated to an unchartable future. Mercifully, few countrymen without dual nationality were able to slip through.

The evacuation at that time was not without incident. A small contingent of Nigerian soldiers who were protecting occupants at the Mammy Yoko Hotel was attacked by the rebels. This attack culminated in the death of a few of the Nigerian soldiers and their subsequent pullback temporarily. Come the turn of the American and French evacuations, they were served by their warships and marines who cordoned off the area, placing marines in the area of operation and patrolling the airspace with helicopters. This was a hair-raising and dramatic display of what governments are there for; they did their nationals proud, putting out such assets to save and protect them. Under civilian control, their armed forces demonstrated a proper universal constitutional function. For our part, we were caught naked even of any means to fight back and defend ourselves. Defenceless before hardliners, but paradoxically cognisant that any such training and equipment of the people by government would have been abused, even by themselves in political violence and persistently in armed robberies and personal vendettas. So that governments should have paid back for their state luxury, their power to appoint their ruling elites (paramountly as handshakes for victory at the next elections), their levying of taxes, their control of state resources by foreseeing these eventualities and adopting policies and programmes to prevent them.

During those early days of the coup d'état, it was difficult to ascertain the feelings of Sierra Leoneans who had never experienced anything of this nature before. There had been uprisings, strikes, and military coups but none to compare with the sobel putsch. Our country does have the singular distinction of changing four heads of state within a week during the first coup that ever happened in March 1967, but still the military-rebel putsch of May 1997 must go down in our history as *the deadliest mother of all coups* and hopefully the last of military adventurism in Sierra Leone. Notwithstanding our experiences with the coups and counter coups, of which our country has had its fair share, this was a time when many countrymen felt disillusioned, disconsolate, and completely trapped in a web of evil. It was difficult to imagine one's feelings after the sobels made the announcement that they had invited the rebels against whom the military had been fighting for over ten years to join them. It was as if we were plunged into an abyss where there was no escape. Imagine being governed by those who had been wreaking havoc in our society, by killing, maiming and pillaging, aspiring to be the new leaders of our fledgling democracy. It was a terrible day when Sankoh was invited to be the deputy head of the sobel junta, and he was heard, or someone who claimed to be him, making a speech, instructing his lieutenants and foot soldiers to come out of the bush and enforce their own form of peace and jungle justice in the city. It was a dark and terrible day indeed.

With their resilience and resoluteness, which were displayed during the peace conference in which military rule with peace before election was vehemently rejected, our countrymen dealt with the dark days of doom in their own admirable way by passive disobedience and a mass exodus out of the country of many professionals. These were people in sensitive positions, those who could not have put up with this intolerable situation and many others from various walks of life. There was a complete and unanimous antipathy to the regime, illustrating the distastefulness of the regime. People just left the country without thinking about the repercussions of living in foreign and strange lands. This was also a time that the miseries of individuals were exploited to the fullest by unscrupulous capitalists. According to the sobels, although the borders, both land and sea, were closed, transporters were not prevented from plying their trade which suddenly became very lucrative, as there was a mad scramble by all and sundry, old and young, the firm and the infirm to flee the country. From this point onwards, it became agony and degradation for those leaving.

There were many horrendous tales about subsequent journeys out of the country and refugee life in foreign countries. Highly placed civil servants struggling to make ends meet in a foreign country; innocent people, especially the old and infirm, dying at sea from the stress of a long and perilous journey; the meagre substance of refugees stolen by the nationals of neighbouring countries.

CHAPTER 4

A CONTINENT STILL DRIFTING

If you believe in the apocalypse, then events in our country are a micro-cosm of the morass in the African continent which portend the doom of the human race. Look at Algeria. While innocent people were being slaughtered because a democratically elected government was proscribed from taking office, the world stood idly by. After much carnage, when it was more difficult to stop the pogrom, only then people began to take notice of the devastation of human lives. Go to Rwanda. For belonging to a different ethnic group, should we say an accident of birth, thousands of innocent victims were slaughtered in cold blood. And the slaughter is still being carried out by militias who were against the Tutsi-led government. But if the Paul Kagami government is today being accused of assassinating dissident journalists in Uganda, the situation becomes murky, bordering on continental despair. For in that objective mind flashes the thought that the accusation that the Tutsis assassinated the crashed Hutu leader, which sparked the genocide, may be true.

Here, we have men ready to kill for power. Liberia has apparently sim-mered down after over twelve years of unwarranted and senseless killing. Angola has left behind it twenty years of civil strife to settle down. The dictator Siad Barre was finally driven out of Somalia, ending many years of oppression, but the country is still unstable with warlords, Islamists, and what you will vying for political control of the country. Meanwhile,

Somaliland broke away, has been apparently enjoying some relative calm, but has yet to be recognised by the international community. In East Africa, Uganda had to endure Idi Amin; they finally got rid of him. And in Kenya, Daniel Arap Moi left office only after nineteen years of misrule. Take Zimbabwe. People are being dispossessed of their land only for the expropriated land to be distributed among party cronies. Those who did not support the ruling party are treated as second-class citizens without the right to redress. Look at the Democratic Republic of Congo. Laurent Kabila was heralded as a liberator. Now the DRC, which went through a rebel war, is more unstable than when it was under the dictator Mobutu.

Watching Rwandan refugees and the displaced trekking over long distances to avoid the carnage in their country, we felt confident and comfortable at the time that such an experience was out of the question as far as Sierra Leone was concerned. We may not have had a similar experience, but many of us were languishing in neighbouring countries as displaced and refugees in strange lands. We were without status: many western countries had simply declared a policy of refusing visas to Sierra Leoneans. And indeed, in some cases when on application for visas from outside Sierra Leone one was described as "stateless," so one did not qualify. Might this be a conspiracy of persecution against Africans?

When are we going to get our act together in Africa? Getting our act together cannot be achieved by inter-tribal wars or inter-territorial confrontations. We may not have a common cause like religion or language to bind us together, as it did for some countries and societies in the past. A caveat, however, is that there are many instances in history when disharmony led to the disintegration and fragmentation of whole nations. In the 1990's decade, we witnessed the fragmentation of Yugoslavia through violent means and the loss of many lives. There was also the case of the USSR, which has now metamorphosed into fifteen states, with Russia still dominant. However, none of these states, not even Russia, wields the considerable power in world politics that the USSR used to wield. As Africans, can't we learn from past and recent history and try to avoid the mistakes made by our so-called peers? Every year international development institutions review world development trends. While other regions of the world get encouraging reviews, Africa's has been dismal and discouraging.

Similarly, when it comes to human rights, Africa leaves much to be desired. From north to south, east to West, the rights of individuals have been violated. Unfortunately, it seems as if some outside forces have been collaborating with Africa's dastardly leaders. The same may have obtained in the West to some extent, but unlike the West, there is no redress in many countries in Africa. The requisite institutions do not exist, they are weak, and/or they are corrupt and toe the line of the perpetrators, usually the governments. In many areas in Africa, to make any progress, one has to be sycophantic.

The system does not allow for independent minds or opposing views. Hence, to perpetuate themselves in power, our political leaders hit on the idea of a system of one-party government. In this system, we are all compelled to be of similar views; therefore, Africa will make rapid political, social, and economic progress. Instead, Africa is making a steady decline, continuing to blame the former imperial powers for our woes. Take Zimbabwe now. Shouldn't it be one of Africa's miracles? But what has it become? Inflation ridden, highly indebted, and high unemployment. Why? Because of the economic mismanagement of Robert Mugabe and his cohorts. To wit, to gain popularity, no matter at what cost, he paid gratuities and pensions to over 50,000 ex-guerrillas by a sum the country could ill afford. Similarly, he has expropriated much of the country's farmlands from white farmers and parcelled them to his cronies, regardless of whether they are farmers or not. Actually, when all is said and done, the West—now apparent champions of democracy, human rights, anti-human trafficking, anti-corruption, and what you will, when these evils are not in their interest, perhaps hoping to expunge their past imperialist misdeeds from the records—should have done much better in world history and in the colonial act that created the problem in the first place. Now all their punitive actions against Mugabe are tacitly appreciated in many African quarters as the revenge of white imperialism against the one who dares. This is the paradox of the African situation. Mugabe, like some African leaders, seems very reluctant to vacate office once power has been tasted.

They want to have a state funeral, so once in the seat of power, only death would prise them from it. What is wrong with many African leaders is, they do not know when to go, even when the tides flow against them. Or are their powers so autocratic and brutal that they fear reprisals? Poverty or penury it cannot be, since from many accounts they usually bleed and ravish their countries' coffers. Look at Mobutu. He was booted out of office and was not even allowed to die peacefully in his own country. He arrogated all his country's wealth, siphoning billions into foreign banks where it would benefit neither his countrymen nor his heirs. President for life Kamuzu Banda is dead. What was all the fuss about? His so-called wealth he left to his lifelong companion. His heirs, his mistress, and the state have been squabbling over his legacy. Nevertheless, lighthouses of hope in the peaceful and democratic transfer of power, amid the turbulent tempest are icons, such as Nelson Mandela and Tabo Mbeki of South Africa, Tejan Kabbah of Sierra Leone, John Kuffour of Ghana, and the rising and serious commitment peer pressure of ECOWAS.

What hypocrites. Our so-called Western friends and allies are all righteousness and indignation at the corruption of African leaders. Forever belittling African countries as banana republics, humiliatingly offering a golden handshake of five million dollars to African leaders to leave power, a lure their debaters say is unattractive, since these leaders can make that in a day. So they cannot plead ignorance that the billions of dollars siphoned into their banks by African leaders are blood money. While condemning these rogues and brigands, they believe that it is their democratic right and free enterprise system not to return these ill-gotten gains to their rightful owners, the poor and downtrodden masses of Africa, but oftentimes to equally corruptly convert them to their own uses. The West points fingers at others but refuses to acknowledge the beam in their own eyes. Can our former colonial master call the kettle black vis-à-vis what happens in the highest institution of their own land?

Paradoxically, it did not stop there. From north to south, Africa has been in turmoil, caused by one thing or the other: if it was not religious, it was ethnic. Even when there was no cause, we had to find something to be fighting for. Was it for recognition or what? And if it was, recognition by

41

whom? The days when countries were building empires have disappeared, dead and gone. Even in Africa, history had told us there were African empires. Do we want to recreate those scenes of the past, not forgetting that it was during those days that our ancestors were sold en masse into slavery and dehumanised. Two hundred years is long enough for us to have shed behind us our slavish mentality.

While we were berating the imperialists for their sins, pointing at the moat in their eyes, we refused to remove the beam in ours. On average after so many years of independence, we are still foundering. Between thirty and forty years ago, many African countries were ahead of Singapore and some other Southeast Asian countries in terms of development. Today you cannot even compare. Singapore has overtaken African countries so many times over. To think that Singapore is a small country on the Malaysian Peninsula, virtually with no known natural resource. In Africa, from north to south, east to West, the continent has abundant natural wealth: oil, fishing, timber, gold, rutile, diamonds, etc. There is no natural resource that cannot be found in Africa, yet the majority of its people remain in abject poverty. Poverty, brought about through the greed, mismanagement, and patronage of its so-called leaders and the open-door policy of African countries towards so-called foreign investors. Unlike foreign investment in Southeast Asia, our crooked politicians only attract foreign investment of dubious origin. Oftentimes knowing the type of systems they operate in, foreign investors seem to take advantage of this to rape African countries, if not with the connivance of African leaders but with their passive approval which is usually paid for by a very fat handshake. Moreover, these are businessmen claiming to be nationals but are of foreign extraction, mainly the Lebanese and Indians. Much as they claim citizenship, they scarcely participate in civic affairs or contribute significantly to community development. When it comes to commerce, they are to be found doing prosperous trade, whether legal or illegal, wholesale and/or retail.

Certainly, they believe they can bribe their way into and out of every situation. The law as far as they are concerned can be flouted with impunity. For them, money talks. A spineless government composed of greedy, shortsighted, and unscrupulous individuals is entirely to blame. These are no other than our corrupt politicians and officials who demean themselves, by their actions to these foreign businessmen. It is not uncommon for a politician, be it a cabinet minister, a parliamentarian or a senior public official, to transact business, whether it is the purchase of merchandise or a service, without paying. His or her "position" in society accords him this right. But of course, this is a cost to the businessman which is easily passed on to the innocent consumer. All those in the vanguard of politics in Africa have as their guiding principle the accumulation of personal wealth at the shortest possible time at the expense of the masses. Indeed, it is shameful that with all its wealth, Africa should depend so much on external sources, often on foreign taxpayers, to support development and training programmes. It is really immoral to be receiving foreign assistance, usually earned from the savings of the donor countries, for the purpose of developing our potential, only for these resources to be diverted to or utilised for the personal aggrandisement of politicians and public officials. How else can one explain the fact that African countries are still undeveloped, given the quantum of overseas development assistance that has been received since the decade of the 1960s? The figure must be astronomical, but this does not correspond to the level of development many African countries have achieved. In fact, the amount of foreign aid poured into Africa runs contrary to its local and national development. By the decade of the eighties, when many countries in Europe, Southeast Asia, and other parts of the world were turning their economies round, many African countries were still in the doldrums. As the international environment became harsher, through massive debt burden and net outflows of capital, the world community, mainly the international donor community, began to notice the plight of underprivileged and deprived Africans. Of course, they had to advance a cause to the ills plaguing African countries. So what did they come up with this time? African countries had suffered the ills of long periods of economic mismanagement coupled with the implementation of inappropriate policies.

Before this period of recession, when many countries in Africa were experiencing reasonable rates of economic growth, institutions like the World Bank and the International Monetary Fund (IMF) were seldom at the vanguard of the continent's development. During this crisis period, these two institutions suddenly assumed the role for policing African economies and putting them back on track. Economic policies suddenly revolved around the jargon structural adjustment, macro-economic stability, privatisation, and the enabling environment. Once this process started, it never stopped; from La Cote d'Ivoire and Ghana to Tanzania and Zimbabwe, almost all states of Africa were under adjustment. Among others, this meant debt rescheduling, currency depreciation, rising prices, distressed public expenditure retrenchment, and divestiture of public corporations' assets. To this day, there is a great divide on the success or failure of structural adjustment programmes, among academics and non-academics alike. It may not be preposterous to state that aid to Africa, originating outside Africa, has sounded the death knell of Africa's initiative, self-esteem, hard work, and inevitably, honesty; now most African governments are classed as corrupt!

After the initial or original SAPS, it was suddenly remembered by the framers and implementers that there were people at the end of these structures, so the human dimension had to be added ex-post. But for all this, unemployment kept rising and more and more people became caught in the poverty trap. And who dared resist the SAPS? Any country having the temerity to resist found itself blacklisted, and an already harsh international economic environment became more hostile. The Bretton Woods Institutions now became more fashionable. How else could one explain the newly industrial countries of Southeast Asia going to these institutions for financial bailouts, countries that were being hailed as the "Asian Miracle" just a couple of years ago? About structural adjustment in Africa, the emerging view was that people continued to suffer when countries were apparently following appropriate economic policies and sound economic management. That was why successive SAPS had poverty reduction programmes attached.

Impoverishment of the masses by their leaders went hand in hand with reducing the ethnic population by slaughter. Again, from north to south, east to west, there was internecine strife. If the cause of strife was not tribal, then it was greed and the quest for power, no matter what method was used to acquire it. One wondered at the multitude of killings that occurred during these times. Ironically, sophisticated weaponry not manufactured in Africa was usually employed, from missiles to AK-47s. Again paradoxically, many of these countries were so poor, and still remain poor, that they could ill afford to feed their own people. Generally, people were and are still starving, children are severely malnourished, health conditions leave much to be desired, and basic service delivery is very much inadequate. Furthermore, any sane individual was left with the impression it was the same "do-gooder" donor countries that offered alms to Africa that provided the arms for such massive destruction. Notwithstanding this state of affairs, African governments or private armies could afford to invest in weapons of mass destruction but could ill afford to feed their people. In effect, while requesting assistance from donor countries, principally from the industrialised nations, for apparently development and training, they spent millions of dollars on purchases of arms and ammunition from these same countries.

Where then is the ethics in all this? At the end of the day, the armament industry is kept running, Africans are killing each other, and they are also starving because their governments cannot afford to feed them. How pathetic. So many of our African leaders are using their own hands to destroy en masse the hands that feed them and put them in power while at the same time keeping the economy of the industrialised nations running, oiled by the sweat and blood of Africans.

Is it any wonder then that Africans are shown the utmost disrespect everywhere? In Europe, from the Iberian Peninsula to the Balkans; in the Americas, from Canada to Chile; and in Asia, from the Middle East to the Far East.

A large number of our leaders have not displayed an iota of integrity in any aspects of their lives. They preach one thing and act in a diametrically opposite manner. In Kenya while both the ruling party and the opposition had criticised an inept electoral commission, when Moi was declared the winner of the then election, there was a change of mood in the ruling party's camp, as the opposition could not make up its mind. The entire exercise was like a charade.

In the West African sub-region, Liberia and Sierra Leone were engaged in a game of cat and mouse and hide-and-seek. To resolve the political crisis in Sierra Leone, Liberia was included as one of the members of the committee of five selected to arbitrate on the raging conflict. (Originally, it was four.) All the time, the role of Liberia, especially of Charles Taylor and his NPFL colleagues, was treated with suspicion as Sankoh and Taylor were close allies. However, since Taylor changed his clothes from those of a warlord to those of an "elected" president, he was perhaps given the benefit of the doubt. It was quite evident, however, when the junta was ousted that the leopard had not changed its spots. Two helicopter loads of the top guns of sobels were intercepted in the Liberia's airspace and forced down by ECOMOG forces stationed there. The fleeing sobels were then apprehended and taken to the ECOMOG base.

As a member of the committee of five, one would have expected Charles Taylor to be happy and satisfied, especially as West Africans in the institution of ECOWAS through ECOMOG succeeded in dislodging a military junta, a feat that had never been accomplished before. The United States went into Somalia to stop factional fighting but failed woefully and retreated in disgrace. The French and the Americans went into Vietnam and had to retrace their steps without achieving their goals. Similarly, the Russians plunged into Afghanistan but left without a single "peace fish" in their nets. Now the United States and Britain disrespectfully rushed the highly respected UN investigator Hans Blix out of the theatre of the investigation to invade Iraq and take out weapons of mass destruction (WMD), which they found nowhere in nine years of occupation. Only bullying world powers could weather such disarming embarrassment, as if it never happened, as the failure of Abu Ghraib never happened to sink their so-called moral high ground. They had to scramble to fall back on regime change, the benevolent surrender of Saddam and his men for execution, and the exit strategy of a "surge" spun and touted as successful, which is actually only a whitewash on rumbling instability. In Iraq as in Afghanistan, where success is always being claimed, the cost of civilian casualties—forget about hearts and minds—is of no concern to the prosecutors of the war. And it is evident from the Afghan war theatre that you have to be extraordinarily gifted warriors like the Taliban. They bring to mind the Viet Cong to endure, chasten, and even overcome the extremely lethal might of NATO. Gaddafi paid with his life for that startling revelation, when the United Nation's 1973 was illegally turned on its head. But there may be Western disillusionment in the offing.

Instead of being proud to be an African for once, Taylor and his government complained about ECOMOG's violation of its territorial integrity. Apparently, he did not realise that Liberia is a constituent part of ECOWAS; furthermore, he was blind to the fact that there were UN and ECOWAS travel bans on the sobels and their sympathisers. The worst that the Liberian government could have done was to have kept silent. Silence would have been golden. In this case, it was the wise thing to do. However, we sympathised with Charles Taylor. After all, he had not yet come to terms with his responsibility of being president of a nation! He did not learn from others' mistakes, so where is he now? His people took up arms against him and drove him not only from the seat of power but out of the country. For his life, he has to thank the Nigerians who maturely spirited him out of the country, in spite of his NPFL massacre of Nigerian citizens in Liberia when ECOMOG peacefully first entered his country.

For far too long African leaders, apart from a few like the late Kwame Nkrumah, have been too parochial and circumscribed in their thinking. The consequences have been far reaching, and this has hampered the progress of the African continent. In the African psyche, instead of thinking as a nation, we think first of the tribe; instead of a region, we think as a country. We never see ourselves as Africans first but only as countrymen, and not as continentals or Africans. Allegiances are so divided. North Africa, mainly Arabic, identifies primarily with the Arab cause, mainly looking towards the Middle East or Arabia. Africa south of the Sahara— that's another matter. There are common causes, but alas, we cannot find a common ground or cause to rally behind. Not even to our historical past. Having gone through a period of colonialism, it would appear that there is a divide, even a great chasm, between those African countries with colonial links with France and those with colonial links with Britain. Indeed, we as Africans have been comfortable with the terms used to describe this difference as francophone and anglophone. Even after so many years of independence, this distinction is still retained. Unfortunately, this goes beyond a mere description in terminology. In negotiating arenas where Africans supposedly come together to seek the common good of the continent, lines of distinction are usually drawn between the francophones and the anglophones. European institutions especially use this divide as a negotiating ploy, either to win concessions from or to hold out giving concessions to Africa.

Plans had already been made in the industrialised countries for greater and better survival and development in the second millennium. Africa should get its act together. Let us utilise and manage our God-given resources properly for the benefit of the people of Africa. After all, the continent contains all of the known and existing natural resources. It is time for us to divest ourselves of the yoke of imperialism on the one hand and bribery, corruption, greed, nepotism, and tribalism on the other. We should be proud of our Africanness and map out our own destiny. With all the resources that we have at our disposal, all the educated brains, we are still requesting technical expertise to show us how to manage our resources and affairs. Often, the experts sent to Africa are no more qualified and are even far less experienced about the local situation than even the "low breed" experts of African nations.

CHAPTER 5

THE FLIGHT

Corpses lying on the road in one of the villages.

After the initial outflow of evacuees, many of whom were foreigners and some Sierra Leoneans with dual citizenship, things more or less settled into a pattern during the term of office of the military junta. Travel agencies, boat owners, and the Road Transport Corporation converted their operations into ferrying Sierra Leoneans "terra marique" through Masiaka, Port Loko, and Kambia into Guinea. Taxi drivers and truck owners also joined in the lucrative exploitation of the woes of a beleaguered nation. The demand for transportation on even unseaworthy barges to Conakry, Guinea, and Banjul, the Gambia, increased steeply. Many people "apparently of substance" were clamouring to travel on deck as long as they would escape from the wanton destruction of Freetown. Some lost their lives by drowning, and in some cases, entire families contributed to the pregnancy of the billows of the sea.

At this point in time, Guinea became a very important orb for many Sierra Leoneans, as a transit point to other West African countries, notably Banjul, Europe, and America, and as a safe haven for many who thought they were leaving the trauma of a chaotic and war situation behind. For many, the sojourn was to have been of short duration as the character of the coup plotters, the response of nationals and the international community and the subsequent behaviour of the sobels did not warrant any serious thinking individual to credit its success for a period of less than a few weeks. As we learnt to our detriment, this was not to be. After reneging on two peace accords and the unwillingness of some of the ECOWAS member countries to use the military option which was the last option, it took nine months to drive the junta from the seat of power. For this, we should be thankful to the vigorous role played by the Nigerians who held the chairmanship of the ECOWAS. After the intransigence displayed by the junta in acceding to the will of the people, it was no small effort made by the then chairman of ECOWAS together with his foreign minister as secretary to the committee of five to put into operation the long-awaited military option.

Getting to Conakry in the Republic of Guinea and also to other provincial areas like Kambia, considered safer than the capital city, was no easy matter. Suddenly, road transportation that was fraught with so many difficulties became quite an affair. In the same way, sea transportation, especially by these *pam pams* (wooden canoes with outboard engines), which was quite hazardous, to say the least, became quite popular. If not for the demand but for the urgency of it, fares suddenly skyrocketed. When it all started, fares were reasonable, but as the realisation that life in the country was becoming more and more hazardous by the minute, fares began creeping upwards while less efficient modes of transportation began plying the route and came into the market. Similarly, travelling by sea on the same journey, the fare trebled while the risk to life because of unseaworthy vessels became very high. Boat owners were not so much particular about the safety of their fare-paying passengers, as they were particular about garnishing super-normal returns on their investments which were old and leaking vessels with neither life-saving equipment nor radio communications. Often, these vessels did not even have compasses. Not perhaps a cause to worry about when one can steer by the stars. Even before the coup of 25 May, traders plying their trade between Guinea and Sierra Leone had lost their lives because their boats had foundered in rough seas of uncharted waters. Come the crises after the coup, boat owners were now braving the seas as far as Banjul in the Gambia.

One can travel by land either by taxi or by bus organised by tour operators or by public corporation buses. Interestingly, fares varied very much. On the tour-operated bus, the official fare was US $50 plus an additional Le10,000 per passenger. Apparently, the Le10,000 was for tips so one could travel from the city to the border without any harassment. By taxi, usually travelling in a Peugeot familiar, the fare was Le25,000 per passenger. Similarly, this fare included a premium for tips against harassment. This mode of transport did not provide for any rebate on the inconvenience factor or nuisance value as again seeking to maximise their profits, taxi drivers would carry ten passengers plus their load, in a vehicle made for carrying seven or eight passengers. Again, the safety of passengers was not an issue; what was essential was the income to be earned from such trips. Of course, in a time of great tribulation, comfort was not of any importance to either the passengers or the taxi drivers. Then there was the Road Transport Corporation bus. The fare charged was Le16,000 from the city to the border. From the border, one was able to get transportation to the nearest country at a cost of about GF10,000, which was equivalent to about Le15,000. After the coup of 25 May, the Sierra Leonean currency the Leone depreciated against the Guinean franc. Previously, the two currencies were almost at par, with the leone sometimes stronger.

Somewhere between the cost of privately arranged transport and the Public Corporation charge must lie the real cost of the transport from the city to Conakry. At the then prevailing rate of Le1,400 to the US dollar, the cost of the tour-operated bus translated to Le80,000 from Freetown to Conakry. That of the Road Transport Corporation bus translated to about Le31,000. Thus between private and public transportation, the rent accrued was astronomical: private transportation was almost three times the cost of public transportation. The implication was that either public transportation was heavily subsidised or the cost of private transportation was too exorbitant. Perhaps the cost by taxi, which worked out at about Le40,000, was the real cost. If this was the case, then government was making a loss of Le9,000 per trip, while the private operator was raking super-normal profits of Le40,000 (a virtual monopoly).

Travelling on private transportation at this exorbitant fare, supposedly including tips and bribes on the way to Conakry, one would have thought one's troubles were over. That of course was a mistake. As soon as you boarded the bus, your troubles started. Even before that. According to the operators, passengers should be at the terminal at 7 a.m. for the bus to leave at 8 a.m. You would have been lucky to depart at 10 a.m. Given the current state of affairs, one had few options. The scheduled days of departure were not regular. At times, there were two weekly runs on Tuesdays and Fridays. For most of the time, only the Friday run was guaranteed. As the sobels found the going difficult, though they could not have enforced border closures, they started imposing constraints on departing passengers. By the end of September 1997, anybody leaving the shores of Sierra Leone had to secure police clearance. Really, this requirement was imposed by another military regime of another era, the National Provisional Ruling Council (NPRC) of 1992. When constitutional order was restored in April 1996, the government never bothered with its removal; whether it was being rigidly enforced was another matter. However, it served the sobels junta's purpose of clamping down on individuals who opposed them vociferously.

To say the least, passengers' first shock was the state and condition of the vehicle, not to mention the overloading. Here again, as private enter-prise demands, the prime motive was profit maximisation. The safety of passengers was not even considered. Assuming the vehicle was road-worthy, other things would follow. How many people lost their lives in trying to flee the trauma in our country? In one instance, when the fighting became so intense that using the regular corridor out of the city became impossible, because of greed, truck operators did not hesitate to use a long-disused road which was hazardous and treacherous. To add insult to injury, vehicles that should have been long consigned to the scrap heap were used. In one such case, over seventy people perished when the vehicle they were travelling on capsized. Apart from the fact that the road was not good, the truck was overloaded. This of course was not a novel phenomenon in Sierra Leone. In fact, life below the poverty line is not new, and not because of poverty and poor and inadequate service delivery. Look at the hillsides in the western area of the country. Private dwellings are springing up and creeping up the hills in a haphazard manner. Look at the wetlands, from east to west. Shantytowns deface the scenery.

As far back as the decade of the seventies, when the country was under one-party rule, days when civil liberties were severely curtailed, when the law was openly flouted by those who thought they belonged to the Establishment and the economy was just starting to get difficult because of corruption and mismanagement, our society lost its soul. The overriding objective was to amass wealth no matter at what cost or whose expense, no matter to what lengths one would go to attain such ends. The degeneracy of our society started around this time. A time when our political leaders were absolutely corrupt depriving the nation of its wealth and raping the masses of their hard-earned earnings left, right, and centre. Chief among the ravishers was the president himself. When Joseph Momoh was manipulated into the position of president in 1985, it was thought that with his military background, discipline would be infused into the national character and there would be a general regeneration of institutional government which had deteriorated under the triumvirate of Stevens, Koroma, and Kamara-Taylor. But no. If anything, the situation got worse under Joseph Momoh. He and his cabal of advisers, many of whom were thought of as educated men, continued to plunder the country. They were so mercenary in their actions that not a single monument, road, school, or a building could attest to their memorial. They plundered, raped, and pillaged. It can be said that the only difference between them and Sankoh's movement was that they did what they did not as rebels but as the government of the day.

Fancy, our country started having energy problems in the late 1970s. By then, load-shedding was intermittent and orderly. As the years went by, the problem of energy turned into a crisis. By the time Stevens' term was coming to an end, the thermal plant was given a facelift instead of being replaced. Meanwhile, after much procrastination, talk of developing hydropower was revived. As early as 1971, a proposal to build a dam at the Bumbuna Falls had been put forward but the APC government was always dragging their feet. Conference after conference was convened to discuss this project, often attended by the ministers and some administrators, but seldom were professionals included. Nothing concrete materialised. Meanwhile, funds were appropriated in the development budget year after year for the carrying out of site works. But as was the modus operandi of the government, the funds got lost somewhere. These funds were never utilised for the purpose they were appropriated. In any case, a project which in 1971 was going to cost the government less than US $60 million by the time it was decided finally to implement it in the late 1980s had appreciated in cost to over US $400 million. After so many postponements, the completion of the dam was scheduled for mid 1998. Alas, Johnny Paul Koroma et al., in their wisdom of wanting to liberate Sierra Leone, our country, by their actions, had by now made this impossible. Before then, it was Sankoh and his rebels who attacked the dam site not once but on several occasions.

Throughout all this period of wrangling and pussyfooting and rebel disturbances, the thermal plant continued to deteriorate. During the time of Joseph Momoh's regime, the city became known as the dark capital, as many areas were without electricity for months without end. In fact, it got so bad that there were times when the entire city was blacked out. Yes, Momoh and his cabal were callous and mercenary, and history will record that during his term of office as president of our country not a single item or event of development occurred. Within this state of affairs, Sierra Leoneans were left leaderless and the ship of state wobbled rudderless in muddied waters. This period could truly be looked upon as one in which anarchy prevailed in our country.

The leadership of the country became so corrupt and incompetent under president Momoh that it became a laughingstock. With all the resources that reside in the country, the Human Development Index (HDI) completed by the United Nations placed Sierra Leone at the bottom of all other countries. What a shame, and since the inception of the compilation of the HDI, our country has been languishing at the bottom. Not by accident, this state of the country was attributed to the war. In truth when the military seized power from Momoh in the early 90s, there were some cosmetic improvements, nothing sustainable or long lasting. With the resurgence of military rule after a brief constitutionality, in May 1997, the country was set back fifty years.

The coup of the Khaki Boys brought euphoria in the country and people went out to dance to welcome the military accession to power. The military junta, which was formed under the acronym NPRC, consisted of a group of young men with an average age of twenty-two years. What a contrast. When a constitutionally elected government was overthrown in 1992, there was great jubilation in the entire country. Five years later, when the same action was repeated, the country mourned and there was widespread condemnation by the international community. The APC party which ascended the throne of power in 1968 under Siaka Stevens was forced out of power by a youthful military regime in 1992. This saw an end to almost a generation of APC misrule and mismanagement.

As usual, to gain our trust, the NPRC, led by Captain Valentine Strasser, promised among other things to end the rebel war, which in 1992 was in its infancy. Being military men, although of tender years, the nation took them seriously and was euphoric at the overthrow of the corrupt Momoh government. To implement their plans, especially those of ending the rebel war, which at that point in time was a low-key affair, the NPRC went on a vigorous and massive recruitment campaign. Unfortunately, those recruited were not properly screened. The majority of them were street and garage boys with no sense of direction, ambition, discipline, or loyalty. They saw the army as a means of enriching themselves through the barrel of the gun. Not surprisingly, when that avenue of amassing wealth was blocked by the installation of a democratically elected government, this group of army boys who thought they had not benefited from the Khaki boys' coup decided to have their turn in plundering the resources of the country. How else could we have explained the return of Captain SAJ Musa, who was a former NPRC strongman expelled because of his rashness and insubordination, aligning himself with the sobel junta? Not only did he align with them, he also took active part in their acts of terror.

All said and done, the NPRC can be faulted for not fulfilling their promise to the nation of ending the rebel war. In fact, as it turned out, events played themselves out during the last days of the Khaki Boys' regime and the subsequent action of the sobel in inviting the rebels to join them in their act of treason, it became clear that the military and the rebels were in cahoots. For a long time, the people of our country harboured suspicions about the military prolonging the war because it was profitable for them. It was even the common belief that the soldiers joined the rebels to terrorise peaceful and innocent villagers just to pillage and enrich themselves. How could we explain the fact that twice, at the end of 1993 and again in 1995 when the rebels were pushed to the corner, the NPRC called for a cease-fire and halted the prosecution of the war? After a month, during which the rebels had regrouped and replenished their arsenal and supply lines, the war recommenced. Who supplied the rebels with arms and ammunition? There were popular stories of contingents of soldiers retreating from rebel attacks, leaving their weaponry behind. There were also stories by captured villagers of military helicopters dropping arms and ammunition in rebel-held territories. Difficult as it was to substantiate, the events of 25 May lent credence to some if not all of these stories. A term which became popular after the escalation of hostilities in 1994 was the word *sobel*, a combination of *soldier* and *rebel*; that was how the soldiers were described by the people who were highly suspicious of the way they were prosecuting the war.

Again, consider, after six years of elusiveness, when Captain Valentine Strasser was toppled in a palace coup by his second in command, Captain

Julius Maada Bio, Sankoh was contacted almost immediately and a conversation between Bio and Sankoh took place, apparently over radio-telephone which was broadcast over the National Radio. At the time, it was highly suspicious. Meanwhile, it was reliably learnt that Bio's sister was a close confidante of Sankoh and high up in the sobel hierarchy. It was hard to imagine that at no time during all these years of war that no communication or contact took place between siblings? That was the "A" side of the coin.

The flip side was difficult to contemplate. Was there any collaboration between brother and sister in pursuing their individual interests? Bio was not just a high-ranking soldier; he was the second in command in the Khaki Boys' hierarchy. The causes and prosecution of the rebel war, military tactics, the rebel movement into and out of villages, and their method of operation were intricate and complex. It was difficult to understand why some people were singled out for execution while others were left alive and why in the same village or area of operation some houses were razed to the ground while others were left untouched. To the sane-thinking countryman, the RUF was not prosecuting an ideological war. Their strategy of killing and maiming innocent civilians went against their propaganda of liberating the people. Perhaps their idea of liberation was to slaughter and maim as many people as possible. Once you are dead, the final solution, you were spared witnessing or suffering from their atrocities.

Like all military regimes, the NPRC was oppressive and abusive of human rights. But in Africa where democracy is yet to take firm hold, civilian regimes are no better. In almost all African countries, those under military rule as well as civilian regimes, the rule of law hardly prevails and the violations of human rights are all pervasive. With corrupt judicial systems that are not independent of the executive, one can seldom seek redress in the courts. Where there is a parliament, it simply echoes the voice of the executive or is just its rubber stamp. Those who claim to be politicians are mostly corrupt as they use their authority or privilege as parliamentarians to enrich their pockets by granting patronage or entering shady deals with rapacious and corrupt businessmen and investors. During the days of the APC government, this was the order of the day. Politics was seen as a way of enhancing the individuals who otherwise would have been nonentities. Those who got elected on fraudulent tickets used this opportunity to ride Mercedes-Benz cars, chased and corrupted young girls, and sold the wealth of the country to shady foreign interests for a mere pittance.

For the period that the Khaki Boys were holding the reins of government, there were the usual stories circulating that they were engaged in intense illegal mining activities. In fact, a story published in one Swedish newspaper and quoted by the *New Breed* newspaper in our country about the involvement of the Chairman of the NPRC, Captain Strasser, in the smuggling of diamonds caused much ado at the time. The editors were locked up and brought to trial and the case dragged on and on. Finally, *a nolle prosequi* was entered by the attorney-general, the case was dropped, and the accused discharged and released.

To do justice to the NPRC regime, young as many of them were, they succeeded in moving forward some aspects of government which had remained moribund during the APC period. Economic reform which was much needed but had been half-heartedly supported by Momoh and his men, and remained shelved for most of the time, was put back on track during the days of the NPRC. Much progress was made in macro-economic stabilisation and creating an enabling environment for private enterprise development. Under a war economy, the NPRC demonstrated its resolve to pursue economic reform and structural adjustment.

To this end, before the escalation of the civil war in 1994, the expectation of achieving the set macro-economic targets like fiscal retrenchment, single-digit inflation, and financial sector reform was very high; to a large extent the economy was well on its way to achieving these targets. Also, in the area of physical infrastructural development, there was commitment to develop a more desirable infrastructure. The thermal generating plant at Kingtom that was in a state of disrepair, only capable of supplying less than 20 per cent of the city's energy demand, was rehabilitated. Indeed, there was a marked improvement in electricity generation to the city when the NPRC was in power. However, one was left wondering whether the problem was only with the machines. There were also problems with management and workers. Disgracefully, government had to hire a foreign consultancy firm to manage the parastatal. Even in times of dire need when the country was strapped for foreign exchange, it was not uncommon for workers to steal the oil, sometimes from the generators. How irresponsible and dishonest can one be? Those who were involved lacked integrity and self-respect. And to imagine that, as impoverished as the country was, the government was paying an undisclosed fee in foreign currency to a foreign firm to manage the corporation. Yet it could not afford the funds to purchase new generators, which were the core of the electricity generation problem in the city.

Putting these three bed mates together (i.e., the APC government under the presidency of Momoh, the big time enjoyer of Lagoonda fame; the Khaki Boys' regime under the chairmanship of Captain Strasser and Brigadier Bio respectively; and the sobel junta under the leadership of Johnny Paul Koroma), there was not much to be said, or to choose from. When stripped of all pretences, they were all ill disciplined and poorly trained military men. Momoh was a failure from beginning to end when he captained the state.

Due to the unpopularity of Momoh's regime, the Khaki Boys, though men—or should one say boys in military uniform—were welcome with open arms by the people. They may even have been well intentioned at the beginning when expectations were very high, but it all turned sour at the end. But for the resolve of the people and the exertion of pressure by some sections of the international community, they wanted to cling to power by fair means or foul. Even their intimidation of the population at the peace conference did not succeed in delivering the decision that they were expecting.

The sobel alliance was a catastrophe from the start. Their modus operandi from the time they seized power transcended the comprehension of sane-thinking people. How could a military which had been fighting an enemy for several years form an alliance to govern those whom they had maimed, pillaged, raped, and killed? It was implicit that the sobel was not strong enough to sustain the coup and that, unlike the Khaki Boys' coup, they were not welcome. Thus to keep themselves in power, they had to govern by terror. The more atrocities they committed, the more the people came to hate and despise them. But they were too insensitive and uncaring to gauge the mood of the citizenry. They tried their utmost to malign the president and tarnish his name. They even co-opted into their ranks an amoral individual like Victor Foh, to cast aspersions on the president, but all to no avail.

When the president was reinstated by the Nigerian-led ECOMOG force, he had the chance to undertake a programme of good governance. The response of the people to his return and reinstatement illustrated the craving for a strong democratic government. The days of partisan politics, sycophancy, and political skulduggery were over. The president is no longer the captive of any party, the Palm Tree in particular. The people of our country amply demonstrated that on his return. The million-dollar question was this: did we as Sierra Leoneans learn any lessons from all that happened during the nine months of junta rule?

CHAPTER 6

CANNOT STOP RUNNING

During the junta days, especially the very early days and the latter days, the road out of the city to Conakry, Guinea, was a transit point and a place of refuge. It was hazardous and expensive. Travelling was not only time consuming but also perilous. In one's haste to vacate the country, the hazard was never given a thought. All one wanted was to leave this hellhole that our country had become. Typically, if you left by road around 10 a.m., you would be fortunate to make Conakry the same day. More often than not, the institutional barriers forced evacuees to sleep either in Kambia on the border or Forecaria on the Guinean side. Truly, travelling from Freetown to Conakry encapsulated the way African countries are governed but also explained the continent's lack of progress and failure to develop and sustain the social and economic livelihood of its peoples.

In the one- or two-day journey from the capital to Conakry, one encountered all the trimmings, institutions, and politics that for so long have been a yoke on our necks. On the Sierra Leone side, after Jui, where the ECOMOG soldiers were stationed, there were over twenty checkpoints manned by rebels who were then the officials and indeed revenue collectors. It was almost a certainty that the money collected was not deposited into the consolidated or any special fund. Considering how much the sobel regime was strapped for cash, these private collections might have been appropriated for salaries and wages of the individual rebel collectors. Imagine what would have stopped these rebels who were now semi-officials of the sobel government unleashing their murderous propensities on

61

fleeing passengers? What should have stopped them thinking that, because these evacuees were not in support of their so-called government, was why they were exiting the country. Had this happened, it was certain no official sanction would have been taken against them.

Perplexingly enough, during the reign of terror of the sobel regime, we never heard or read about a single voice raised or a single line written by any human rights organisation condemning the acts of these monsters; nor was any disciplinary action taken against human rights violations by the powers that be. As documented in the TRC report, the worst punishment meted out to these culprits was for them to be transferred to another area, to continue as ever before. This is in conformity with the historical policy of recycling "old hands" even when they are found wanting. Even when these very same people took up arms against the students when they wanted to exercise their democratic right, killed some of them, human rights organisations were silent on the matter. Now, after the overthrow of the hateful military junta and subsequent arrests of some of the ringleaders, human rights organisations suddenly became vocal. How ironic! Sometimes, one wonders about the mind-set of these organisations. It is well and good to sit in their ivory towers in luxurious surroundings and pontificate about the apparent crimes of others.

Coming back to our so-called officials at the various checkpoints on the road to Kambia, thankfully they never thought of committing any acts of aggression against travellers, save only relieving them of their meagre resources. But then at the travel agency, we were assured of a safe passage through as all had been arranged, the reason why the cost of the journey was very expensive. According to the agents, the Le10,000 per passenger was to ensure a hazard-free passage to Conakry. Under these prevailing circumstances, getting to Conakry was no child's play. When somebody, looking heavily drugged, is waving a gun at you, you would want to keep any altercation to the barest minimum. Although arrangements had been made apparently beforehand for free movement of passengers, more money had to be paid to facilitate vehicular movements beyond these checkpoints. In the midst of all this, arguments sometimes ensued among the sobels themselves whether vehicles should be allowed to proceed. These arguments were not only protracted but also threatening and risky to innocent passengers. However, this was a time when sobel minions acting as officials had the opportunity to demonstrate their authority.

The first impediment was at the first checkpoint, where all the passengers had to alight from the vehicle and file past an official in civilian attire who could barely read or write. His function? To take down the names and numbers of police clearance of travellers. With the disorganisation and disorder of junta rule, one could imagine how time consuming and ominous this exercise was. At the time, it was no concern to those leaving of what the essence of the taking down of names was. Reflecting on the carnage that trailed the junta forces during their violent and disgraceful dislodgement from power, they probably had a hidden agenda that bordered on evil. If they had not been removed from power, one option they might have followed was the extermination of those who had left but had to return, as sojourning in a foreign land on meagre resources would have been unsustainable.

Getting to Jui where the ECOMOG forces were stationed, there were road blocks but the presence of the ECOMOG soldiers was not that visible, and crossing was not a problem; the bus was not stopped, nor were the passengers checked. From that point on, it was smooth sailing until we arrived at mile 38, an area not far from the gateway to the provinces. There we were again confronted with confusion at the checkpoint manned by sobel soldiers and policemen. Between the soldiers and the policemen manning the checkpoint, they could not decide where the vehicle should be parked, so an argument ensued. In fact, the policemen had the last say as they decided the bus should have stopped so many yards before the checkpoint. The driver had to reverse to comply with this instruction. Hey, presto! After the usual greasing of the palm, the bus was allowed to proceed. This palm greasing was expected at every checkpoint manned by the sobels. Without it, one could not be allowed to proceed. Surprisingly, at Masiaka, or mile 47, although the sobel presence was heavy, very little difficulty was encountered and the passage was smooth. Passengers did not even have to alight from the bus, but of course, the usual passport had to be tendered—palm greasing. This point also marked the end of any stretch of good road, up to Forecaria. Consequently, the ride after Masiaka became more uncomfortable and considerably slower.

By whatever yardstick used, Sierra Leone is a small country. Consequently, with all its potential resources, proper management should have ensured an enviable infrastructure, but it is a disgrace that the country cannot boast of any good stretch of road of class "A" standard. We are content with substandard in all aspects of our life. Even when something is mediocre by all standards, one would hear sections of society, and a considerable one at that, showering plaudits on all and sundry. Imagine the road that takes one to the diamond-rich areas of the country being in a considerable state of disrepair. That is shameful and disgraceful, but perhaps not more so than the deplorable conditions that exist in these mining areas themselves. Truly, mining is an extracting industry; in our country, it is a question of exploiting these resources without a thought of investing in these very areas or even the people of these mining towns. What a disgrace! But just consider this: how would investment occur in these places? Of course, there will be no investment when the bulk of the industry is in the hands of, or controlled by, people who are not indigenous to those areas. More precisely, they are likely foreigners of dubious character who are only interested in plundering the country's wealth. Successive governments from the time of Siaka Stevens up to now, even including the military regimes, have been responsible for this state of affairs. Foreigners bribed to get mining licences and then smuggled the gems out of the country, in most cases aided by corrupt government officials. Why? Just for the few thousands of leones or United States dollars that would be dished out. These corrupt officials are either too greedy or short-sighted to count the economic and social costs incurred by the country by what they regard as a simple transaction. How lamentable is the fate of our country. Successive regimes have indeed committed treasonable acts against the people of this country. The military boys of course seized on the opportunity to stage coup d'état but—wonder of wonders—once they held the reins of power, they also contracted this disease of greed and corruption in no time. The object of their greed became the diamonds. And to think that diamond is about the strongest and purest element. Perhaps that is why men of lesser characters seek to possess it, no matter the cost.

Returning to our journey from the country, apart from the bumpiness of the road, travelling was trouble free up to Port Loko. After Masiaka, where the road network diverges, to the north, onwards to Guinea and the south and east, onwards to Liberia and Guinea, there were fewer checkpoints. But getting to Port Loko itself was much of a relief. It is a large town and the presence of soldiers and rebels was not much in evidence. However, no stop was made for a rest or for stretching one's cramped legs, but the journey continued to the next major post on the way to Conakry being Kambia, where also there was a customs post.

Before arriving in Kambia, there was one checkpoint manned not only by soldiers and police but also by civilians. Once this post was reached, all passengers in the bus had to disembark and were interviewed. But before that, every passport was collected and examined. If you were travelling after the student demonstration in September, it would do you no amount of good if you were a teacher. There occurred an incident in which one of the passengers had written on his passport "Economist" as his profession. As soon as one of the interrogators saw this, he immediately accused the passenger of being a teacher and therefore a traitor to the cause of the AFRC-RUF. There followed a long session of interrogation during which it was painstakingly explained to the interrogator that it was not only in the classroom one would find an economist. In fact, it was made crystal clear that economists would scarcely be found in classrooms. Thankfully, this explanation proved convincing and the said passenger was allowed to proceed.

Pity the countrymen who were put to considerable ridicule by the AFRC-RUF and their sympathisers. During the entire affair, apart from the fear that was inflicted on the nation, many of us felt ashamed to be cast in a similar cloth, especially when people like Dr John Karefa-Smart (now late) and former president Momoh (now also deceased) sympathised with their cause while others like Dr Wiltshire Johnson (now late) and Pallo Bangurah gave them advice.

It is axiomatic that the longest road has a turning, but by December 1997, the question or worry in the minds of numerous Sierra Leoneans was not when the tide would turn but when would it all end, and end it did. Even those who fled the shores of Sierra Leone, their physical journey did come to an end, once in the county of refuge and finally when they returned home after the disgraceful booting out of the sobel junta.

Many Sierra Leoneans stayed in Guinea during the junta interregnum, some went as far as the United States of America, others to parts of Europe, but West Africa was host to the largest number of refugees. Experiences varied from country to country and between those in camps and those who were not in camps. It would be difficult to pass judgment on the official treatment meted out by some West African countries on the refugees; any judgment passed by those of us who sought refuge in these countries was bound to be emotionally coloured. However, on a more personal basis, those of us who were lucky to be housed and cared for by families in Ghana, Nigeria, and the Gambia have nothing but gratitude and praise for these individual families. Some of these families were so hospitable and understanding that we felt very much at home and part of the family. Perhaps these were the lucky few; majority of those who left the shores of Sierra Leone were not so fortunate. One thing was clear though: our country is a paradise to all and sundry. In everything, the nationals of those countries came first: in business, in schools, and in hospitals. Indeed, in all walks of life, their nationals were given pride of place. They were treated with deference and like princes. But who would complain? Definitely not the Gambian, the Ghanaian, or the Nigerian. Even when a decision was taken against foreigners, somehow or the other, it was seldom enforced; somewhere in the chain, from law enactment to enforcement, there was a link that was broken.

The plight of those seeking refuge in neighbouring Guinea and other countries was rather mixed. In most cases, it was intolerable; as the saying goes, beggars have no choice. It was pathetic to witness Sierra Leoneans, the high and mighty, and the lowly and humble, queuing for food at the embassy's premises every day, looking haggard and forlorn. Those who managed to secure houses were charged astronomical rent for very basic accommodation. And still, those traversing Guinea by land to places like the Ivory Coast and Ghana were harassed every part of the way. There were so many checkpoints, and at each checkpoint, one was not allowed to proceed without paying some sort of "tax." At this crisis time, this behaviour seemed heartless to many of the travellers. We talk of African Unity and social integration. ECOWAS has been in this for ages, but have we changed? A friend in need is a friend indeed. Guinea harboured many Sierra Leoneans, but at what cost? Many who travelled to that country by road lost almost all of their meagre possessions by the time they arrived at their destinations. At the border, before one's passport was stamped, money had to be exchanged with the responsible officials. That was after Guinean soldiers manning the border post had "liberated" travellers of their finances, on the pretext that they had no foreign exchange clearance certificate. As if at these calamitous times that was possible. Also, getting to Conakry was no child's play, as the rite of passage was secured at the many checkpoints by again money changing hands!

CHAPTER 7

TRANSIENT LEGITIMACY

**Highway in Kono where some women came
out to talk peace with the rebels.**

God moves in a mysterious way, His wonders to perform. What more proof do we, nationals of Sierra Leone, need after the way the unholy rebel-military alliance was ignominiously booted out of the seat of power? When the Conakry Peace Accord was signed, apparently legitimising the unholy military junta for six months, many of us were greatly troubled. For us the unthinkable had happened, allowing the butchers to continue wreaking their atrocities on innocent men and women and children for another six months. It was as if the sky had fallen in on us.

As it turned out, our worst fears were realised. On the night of the signing of the accord, the entire country witnessed an intense shooting spree by the soldiers and rebels, their own way of celebrating their Pyrrhic victory. For the majority of countrymen, especially those in country, it was the beginning of another period of woe as the junta thought that they now had the legitimate right and therefore the licence to do whatever they fancied.

The mayhem and terror unleashed by them were a new experience for us. Perhaps all this grief would have been spared had ECOMOG invaded much earlier, say in August after the second Abuja debacle. We could only speculate. We were all hoodwinked into believing that these military boys would defend their, not our, territorial integrity to their last drop of blood. Late Corporal Sankoh made that proclamation, so also did Territorial Integrity and others, but when the day of reckoning came, they fled with their tails between their legs. In any case, where are they today, *these extremely patriotic citizens* who were going to fight to the last drop of their blood? They have been consigned to Hades.

Although the junta was given six months to return the reins of power to the constitutionally elected government, that was not to be. They themselves brought on their own demise sooner rather than was expected. Considering the weapons that they had amassed, we should thank the good Lord that they neither had the time to implement their dastardly plans nor the expertise to use some of the weapons.

They were given the opportunity to vacate the seat of power peacefully. But no! They were too greedy. From the onset, they were given the option that their former peers, the NPRC Boys had, but they turned it down. Apparently in Africa, once power is tasted, it is difficult to surrender to the democratic process. Due to their intransigence, they were given an ultimatum by ECOWAS, but again they had their "enlightened comrades," the likes of Momoh, Karefa-Smart, and Victor Foh, who thought they were experts in the English language and advised that the absence of a punctuation mark could change the entire sense in the communiqué that was issued. Exercising patience, ECOWAS called another meeting, this time cleaning whatever cobwebs were in the minds of the likes of Captain Gborie, but again this advice fell on deaf ears.

By and large, while the junta thought they now had the making of an acceptable regime, instead of conserving the relatively scarce resources that they had to bring some sanity to their tyrannical rule, they used whatever resources they had illegally acquired to stockpile arms. According to some of the testimonies in the TRC report, they used the proceeds from diamond sales and agricultural produce, forcefully acquired from local inhabitants, and illegal mining to finance arms purchases. Yet all the time that ECOMOG was trying to enforce the embargo on ships that were apparently transporting these arms, the regime was crying foul, putting out to the world at large that they were bringing in rice, wanting to mobilise opposition against the ECOMOG. To some extent as far as the local population was concerned, this ploy succeeded, especially as people's existence was very precarious, seemingly blaming the ECOMOG for the hard times in the country. As one of the victims of the junta's misrule, I was perplexed at people's misplaced anger or blame. Ironically, those at the time who were demonstrating against the ECOMOG, especially Nigeria, went as far as to inscribe on one of the main thoroughfares in the centre of the city their repugnance to the ECOMOG forces, an inscription which was still there after our country was liberated in February by the very ECOMOG intervention force. After February, it was all a big welcome and thank-you to the ECOMOG force that was no longer seen as interventionists but liberators.

CHAPTER 8

RETURN FROM EXILE

Some amputee victims of the rebel war.

After the inglorious exit of the rebels in February 1998, the constitutionally elected government triumphantly returned to Freetown amid much
jubilation and fanfare. President Ahmad Tejan Kabbah appointed a new
cabinet considerably leaner, not necessarily more efficient and/or effective.
From the point of view that many of the old hands who proved ineffec-
tual and corrupt in the previous government were recycled into the newly

constituted cabinet did not allay people's fears that it was going to be business as usual. He did establish a policy advisory unit, but its mandate did not appear to be clearly spelt out and many a time was in confrontation with the cabinet. Work was mired in the usurpation of cabinet's authority and trivialities.

Second time around, the feeling conveyed to the public by the actions or inaction of the SLPP government was one of weakness compounded by the act of floating aimlessly in a deep and perilous sea.

The honeymoon over, it was back to the stark realities of life in a battered, impoverished, and war-torn country. The resources of both the public and private sectors, including households, were all but wiped out. During the period of conflict, and especially after the wilful destruction of productive and social infrastructure, local and foreign investors were driven away. Many industries, including those that were driving growth, were vandalised, not to talk of the destruction to basic infrastructure that was already inadequate to create the enabling environment to attract foreign direct investment. Government could not even finance its daily operations as its sources of revenue had completely dried up, either through vandalism by the rebels or the inability to generate taxes from the commercial sector. Current thinking then was that our country needed all the help it could get from the international donor community, and cap in hand, begging we went. Indeed, the donor community was very sympathetic to the cause of this small country which had sacrificed so much just to preserve its budding democracy. The British, the Americans, and the Dutch all apparently came to our aid. The United Nations of course made its own contributions, among which was the observer mission consisting of about one hundred military and other personnel. All this was well and good. Those Western nations steeped in the tenets of democracy were not going to allow a bunch of misguided individuals to subvert the principles of democracy for which so many of them had fought so hard, and for which our country was marking its footsteps.

At the time, we were all so euphoric about coming back to a distressed, but freer environment that nobody questioned the aims and objectives of these donors. Apparently, their aims were altruistic. Being a sceptic, I do not believe that for one minute, but it is only a point of view which may or may not correspond to the truth, which in itself may not be absolute but a matter of perception. Certain things which were evident in the way and manner that this assistance was administered and distributed perhaps leaves no doubt as to the major beneficiary. Certainly, the people were only pawns in the game of donor, especially bilateral donors, assistance to the developing world, mainly sub-Saharan Africa.

In the case of aid administration and distribution, the British government, through its development arm Department for International Development (DFID), and the United Nations Trust Fund set up for Sierra Leone and utilised to finance the UN observer mission, DFID did a good job by putting so large a volume of resources into the demobilisation programme for ex-combatants, but alas, they had to recruit an expert team from abroad to execute the programme. We can speculate on the nationality of the team that was recruited for this purpose. It would be most informative to know what percentage of the total aid package was recovered by the donor in the form of wages and allowances. However, the initial phase of the DDR programme was bogged down in administrative trivialities, poor interpersonal relationships, and incompetence. In the final analysis, the DDR programme was accomplished by Sierra Leoneans, who manned all aspects of the programme and stations in the country.

In the case of UNOMSIL, as the observer mission was known, we may not query the quantum of resources paid as salaries, allowances, and re-imbursables. What was so visible was the number of Toyota Land Cruisers that they were driving around. To a country boy like me, it appeared as if each member of the mission had one Land Cruiser and more. Just for the fun of it, to an impoverished and battered economy like ours, it should make interesting reading to calculate the relative share of the total cost of these Land Cruisers in the nation's gross national product. However, one should not complain too much as there were other economic gains, especially those accrued to property owners, barkeepers, and the like. And to think that these people were here specifically to observe the situation, interpreted to mean not only to supervise the peace, but as soon as there were rumours of a rebel invasion of the city, they were all evacuated. Who would blame them? They were too "precious" to lose.

After the epic of March 1998 and the return of some amount of sanity to the populace, the law began to take its course and justice was seen to be done. Many of the coup plotters and their accomplices were charged to court and court proceedings began in the magistrate courts then moved to the high court all of which are located in the city centre. After braving nine months of junta misrule, the public had to put up with the inconvenience of not using the main thorough fares of the city as they were blocked to vehicular and pedestrian traffic, again all for the junta. This went on for quite a period of time. During this period, travelling to and from the centre of town was a nightmare for many as the options available were not adequate to carry the volume of traffic that was being diverted onto them. Mornings especially were chaotic, to say the least, with considerable loss of time and resources.

Eventually, the trials came to an end with the majority of the accused sentenced to death. Those who were tried by court-martial and sentenced to death have had their sentences carried out. Those who were found guilty and sentenced in the civil courts appealed against their sentences. Yet the "play" did not end there. The chief perpetrator was also under sentence of death, but there was talk of his release. To crown it all, the major players, like Johnny Paul, who was one-time head of state, were still at large. Yet the megalomaniac parasitic mosquito who thought that murdering innocent civilians was a passport to fame was still at large and causing the people of this country so much grief and distress.

The restitution of constitutional rule saw the mobilisation of the masses. In no time at all, the city was cleaned up and the junta misrule became a thing of the past, or did it? This period saw also the untimely deaths of many Sierra Leoneans, both young and old, women as well as children, firm and infirm, as the longer-term effects of nine months of continuous strain and stress began to take their toll. People died suddenly, leaving to speculation the cause of death. That apart even the government had not really demonstrated that will and commitment to look after its people. It kept harping on the destruction of its revenue base, the lack of resources, and what have you. But in the face of all this, it was able to afford to house the bigwigs like the VP in expensive hotels for as long as it was desired and spent billions of leones to rehabilitate ministerial quarters, while the bulk of the population was and is still homeless and unemployed. Many others had lost their homes.

During this period, when some radical shift in traditional orthodoxy was required, the government came out with no clear policy as to the direction it chose to move the economy. For example, in the midst of the persistent rebel crisis, whereby it was established that certain foreign countries in the sub-region were actively involved in destabilising the country, no clear foreign policy was designed even to deal with this problem. Also in the context of ECOWAS which took the leading role in restoring democracy, we never heard of our president visiting other heads of state like Jerry Rawlings of Ghana or even Blaise Campaore of Burkina Faso; all his shuttling was between Conakry and Abuja. Considering the resource constraints operating on the ECOWAS states, a personal visit might have made all the difference. This having been said, it cannot be gainsaid that Nigeria, which had taken the leadership role in the military and political spheres, did an excellent job and one would be remiss in not commending them for that. Contrary to popular thinking, the question then was not what was in it for them but how much control the president or the people of their country had over their own policies. Of course, the optimistic view was that the situation would have been under control by then; pessimistically, the sobels, considering their intransigence, abilities, and sponsors, might regroup and start the destabilising process all over again. This of course was not a case for dialogue but one for government to consider its options carefully and sagely.

It was highly questionable whether the government then had the will, the courage, and wisdom to carry the day in this conflict. If the past record was anything to go by, the signs of the times did not augur well for the nation. We could not have said that the government demonstrated the resolve to tackle what appeared to the nation, simple problems, let alone something that was considered more complex. From the onset of the rebel war, right on to the military interregnum, the government propaganda machinery left much to be desired. It appeared that the government did not fully realise the importance of information and also sensitisation and communication. We should have taken a leaf out of the sobels' book. Our government lost the propaganda war. It was even our hope that they would not also lose the military battle. Unfortunately, our government seemed to have lost so many other battles: the war on poverty, the war on greed and corruption, the war on massive pilfering of public funds, the war on ineffective decision-making, the war on general mismanagement, and the war on indiscipline and disregard for the law. One could go on and on.

Given this new dispensation, the general attitude of the people of our country was lambasted by all and sundry in the electronic and print media. Did this outcry for a change of attitude make any difference? Government together with the international community invented programmes like Good Governance and Awareness Raising, programmes that were supposed to change people's attitude, but all was to no avail. Not surprisingly, certain values can only be inculcated within the family setup and over a period of time, and these are best assimilated when the child is young and tender. As the good book says, train up a child the way he should go and he will never depart from it. Programmes that were being undertaken by the National Commission for Democracy and Human Rights (NCDHR) could have achieved greater and longer-lasting results had children been taught their civic duties from their school days. In addition, if those holding the reins of power do not lead unequivocally by example, it will be virtually impossible to instil values it does not possess.

Be this as it may, our country was caught in a web that seemingly it could not break. A large portion of the public believed that the elected government was incapable of taking any meaningful decision. Rumour also had it that the old guard of the ruling SLPP still believed that they should continue to be the vanguard of the party, and many a time they felt excluded from the decision-making process by the executive. Similarly, many a time the legislative arm of government felt they were being railroaded by the executive. To add to this concoction, it was even rumoured that the principle of collective responsibility was sometimes anathema to cabinet.

Where did this leave this poor and war-beleaguered country? Small wonder that even its citizens did not take the government seriously. Regulations were openly flouted because we had come to realise that we were living in a society where there was no redress. It was popularly said that the law is no respecter of persons. Alas not in our country! The more affluent one was, the more political clout one wielded. This was the unfortunate situation we found in this seemingly new dispensation. Was the authority powerless to act? Of course, it was as if they were the ones who blazed the trail of indiscipline. Give a man some authority in our country and he begins to think that it is a licence to flout the law generally, or to feel he is above the law. What anarchy!

One of the consequences of all this was the level of indiscipline that prevailed in all levels of society: in the offices, in the schools, in the homes, even in the forces, which were usually the last bastions to collapse because of their hierarchical structures. Unfortunately, if this general collapse was noticed, the government proved incapable as always to address the problem. There was always a so-called VIP who would hold brief for any of these perpetrators. For example, so many attempts were made to rid the capital's main thoroughfares of street trading, but that scarcely succeeded as these very so-called politicians would plead for their people. Instead, the situation got out of hand, as many more streets in the business district came under street trading. For example, in one of the streets that building materials stores predominate, necessitating parking space for heavy trucks, the entire length has been commandeered for street trading. For political reasons, or so it is said, the authorities are powerless to act. In our country, private and indeed selfish interest supersedes public good. We have a convoluted process of thought. In all aspects of life, that quality of justice and sense of fair play were suborned by the very authority themselves.

While in exile during the interregnum, so much passion was poured into turning over a new leaf once we returned, but our memory is so short that it took us no time at all to return to the old ways. It was business as usual, not only the government but even the public at large. No sooner than we were back in the country, we started reading about massive corruption and fraud in official circles. Yet it never struck people, or perhaps our society is so insensitive that this country could ill afford the pillaging of government coffers. While millions of public funds were and are still illicitly being siphoned away by a few profligates, the very government could not afford to pay staff members' salaries. What an anomaly! While government complained of being resource inebriated and expected the donor community to provide the shortfall and more for the implementation of programmes, some mercenary groups of private individuals cosily, without any fear of retribution, converted millions of government funds into private accounts! The government was taking action as usual but nothing tangible emerged. Oh yes, these peccadilloes are revealed and much hullabaloo is made by public officials. But wait for it. Yes, you got it right. Action was only seen to be taken, which for this government was a very long and tedious process. As had been proven time and again, our country was one where the due process of the law must take its course and ours is a fledgling democracy. But perhaps it is because of this that we have to be careful not to send the wrong signals to the world community in order not to offend those who apparently provide us with aid to carry out the business of government.

Since the return to democracy in 1996, when the government effectively embarked on a programme of reconstruction, we have been overly dependent on foreign assistance to undertake our reconstruction programme. However, it never occurred to the powers that be that much more would have been achieved if a national fund for the reconstruction exercise had been launched by government in which households, companies, and the like would have invested, if not for the quantum but to illustrate to the donor community that the government specifically and Sierra Leoneans in general were committed to their own welfare. But no, we are so poor that the thought was unthinkable. Really are we so poor that of a population of five million we cannot afford to contribute Le100 per head which could have yielded Le500 million to be used as leverage to attract other funds? Even though this is not done, we complain when bilateral donors dish out their funds to their own NGOs. With our short memories, we also forget about the articles littering our daily newspapers about the profligate manner government money is frittered away.

The civil war was over. General and local elections had been held, UNAMSIL had started handing over security to our local security forces, but our government seemed to be floundering in a deep ocean. Indeed, it sometimes gave the impression that it leapt before it looked. Not only that, when serious mistakes were made, nobody had the temerity to explain, let alone try to reverse these mistakes. Even with vociferous public outcry, we were treated as fools or just quietly ignored with the hope probably on the part of government that it would go away; just like the ostrich burying its head in the sand to get rid of the prey. Take the case of our parastatals. Recommendations were made about the running of some of them, but did the government act on them? No! What about the fraudulent misuse of public money? Was there any prosecution let alone conviction? No! What about the prolonged civil strife? ECOMOG always complained about the unfulfilled pledges of other ECOWAS member states. Did our government mount any vigorous canvassing of other heads of states to get them to redeem their pledges? No. Somehow, our country was consistently receiving bad press abroad, but did the government mount any counter measures to improve the country's image abroad? No!

We could go on and on because this indecisive behaviour has been a feature of this government since it took office in 1996. It was our fervent hope that with the new dispensation things would change, as we were all expected to have learnt our lesson from the catastrophic events of 1997. But no, we did not, and where has that taken us? Into a worse mess, a situation that was beyond human comprehension. But wait. We should not be hasty in our condemnation. Perhaps what happened was beyond the comprehension of those who suffered but not those within the corridors of power; most of them, either by accident or by design were afforded protection by the security forces or carted abroad in haste to preserve their precious lives as they were indispensable

CHAPTER 9

THE FIRST REBEL INCURSION INTO FREETOWN

Burnt carcase of one of the country's traditional
landmarks, "the Big Market" in Freetown.

The sixth of January 1999 was a fateful day in the annals of the history of our country when rebels overran the capital city. That day, outside the normal run of time, the city slid down into an underworld of atavistic and hellish horrors, indiscriminately unleashed by a callous, unruly horde on an already traumatised people. An entire city was subjugated under inhuman acts of brutality, culminating in the wanton destruction of both life and property. These rebels who in actual fact were the disbanded soldiers of the Sierra Leone Army who had been living in the jungle for years forcefully marched on to the corridors of power, thinking that by force of arms they could govern a nation that in the recent past was looked upon as the Athens of West Africa.

But that was not the worst of it. There have been military coups in our country before, but at no time, before 25 May 1997 and 6 January 1999, was the civilian population so overtly and comprehensively betrayed by the soldiers who took an oath to protect not only our territorial integrity but also the safety of the civilian population against all acts of aggression. Ironically, as events unfolded on a day that happened to be African Liberation Day, our soldiers turned their weapons upon us. They threw off their constitutional and theoretical cover, which they never really assimilated, for what they really were. The civilian population had to toe the line. Our human rights were severely trampled upon. It was a case of being compliant and surviving like a slave or being stubborn and dying like dogs. These people who joyously proclaimed a military junta under the nickname *sobels* did not waste any time in seeking to redistribute wealth by unorthodox strategies. They "legalised" looting and pillaging of the entire civilian population. They even had the temerity to attack all the prisons in the country, releasing convicted criminals, all in the name of liberation and a continuation of the struggle. This was the design of rebel leader Corporal Foday Sankoh, now a statistic, in a struggle against whom or what only Sankoh and his cohorts knew. In their drugged, befuddled minds, they probably saw themselves as the saviours of the underprivileged, in this instance, those who like them were dropouts, drug addicts, thieves, and ne'er-do-wells. Never before in the history of a nation had the wise been governed by such a group of riff-raff.

History is littered with regimes of bloodthirsty men, following the principles of Machiavelli, who however employed their intellect or cunning to enforce their rule, but not with low-classed, absolutely senseless men, devoid of stature other than the gun and the drug marijuana or cocaine.

How could the running of a country by men and boys who were always in *cloud nine* and thinking that the seat of power is paradise? What a travesty of religion and morality where the daily prayers of unscrupulous characters are said with the conviction that they legitimised their heinous crimes and endeared them to the oppressed nation! If not suffering from delusions, how could a so-called head of state broadcast to an entire nation that he had made a covenant committing the nation to God? In his confused state of mind, Johnny Paul Koroma must have thought the charade over the radio absolved him from his sins. According to the Bible, blasphemy is a sin unto death. He being religious should be reflecting on this.

On the other hand, religious groups should beware the destructive abuse of our national, religious tolerance, for which, without poisonous, foreign mischief, we are naturally second to none in the world. Poverty and disillusionment over one thing or another have spawned an overgrowth of unprincipled and even evil religious groups nationwide cunningly pursuing wealth—some infiltrating politics. It is an evil religion of the three witches of Shakespeare's archetypal *Macbeth* that prophesied to Johnny Paul Koroma that it was his destiny to rule Sierra Leone. As a soldier, like Macbeth, he sought the shortest cut to political power, only to petrify his soul in the bosom of evil.

The rebels met their Waterloo when they got to Freetown. While fighting in the provinces, for close to eleven years, they rationalised and excused their crimes by claiming they were only sending messages to the government. For this, they killed; maimed; raped; burnt down entire villages; and pillaged the property of innocent men, women, and children who in their simplicity and trustworthiness knew little or nothing at all about government. All they wanted was to be left alone to earn their livelihood, bring up their families, and in their own small way, contribute to community development. But no! That was not to be. Sankoh and indeed his benefactors in the sub-region thought they could play God by the violent disruption of the lives of these people. Perhaps Foday Sankoh saw himself as the Moses of our country. Indeed, how ironical, seeing that many a time modern charismatic religious groups (sects) had likened the nation to the children of Israel. Again, He should bless the incompetent Momoh against whom he started his "liberation struggle." Although he had been included in the peace process, not because of his fame but because of his notoriety, we normal and sane-thinking countrymen and women could find gratification in the annals of history. Posterity will unmask Sankoh for the monster and megalomaniac that he was. Only, it was unimaginable that some of those who claimed to be rational (some power brokers) did not see him for what he was. Perhaps they were all propelled by the same lusts and appetites, being of different colours but of the same ilk.

Although the rebels had been in the city previously, when invited by the sobels this time round, the context and environment were different. The distinction then was they were invited by the sobels to form an unholy alliance. This time round, the jungle boys were not invited but came in the guise of peace. "The military assault" on the capital city Freetown quickly evolved into one of the most concentrated spates of human rights abuse and atrocities against civilians perpetrated by any group or groups during the entire history of the conflict. Possibly, they were invited by their collaborators who turned out to be all over the city and in places of position. History will tell. What is clear was the sheer incompetence of the state intelligence apparatus in allowing the invasion to happen. Ample evidence in the TRC report testifies to the fact that the rebels were going to attack Freetown, and this was no secret to the authorities.

Not long before this invasion, self-styled General Sam Bockarie, alias Maskita, had proclaimed that the rebels would be coming to Freetown with the aim of rendering the country ungovernable. Some people who perhaps knew the psyche of the rebel gave credence to this proclamation while others thought of it as an idle threat, especially as not only was there an ECOMOG presence in the city but their headquarters was now based in Sierra Leone. Unfortunately, as has been attested, key strategic positions on the path to Freetown were left exposed or abandoned by

ECOMOG soldiers. Theoretically, one might have argued that with the presence of ECOMOG, Maskita would not dare invade the city, but he did and unfortunately succeeded in carrying out his threat of making the country ungovernable. Being who he was, he might not have known it, but he more than succeeded. Normal life was destabilised and we could not even predict when it would return to normal. As the situation warranted, life as we used to experience it before this invasion has not been the same. Perhaps that may be for the better. At the time, the city was delineated into over one hundred zones with related security checkpoints manned by Civil Security Movements (CSM).

Considering the pain we suffered, it is time for Sierra Leoneans to accord to security the importance that it deserves. We have all been traumatised, because of our complacency; after March 1998, security was not taken seriously, by both the government and the people. Only lip service was paid to securing the safety of the nation; for that single lapse, we have paid dearly with our limbs, lives, and property.

Alas! The populace was given a rude awakening on that fateful morning, the sixth of January. Before this apocalyptic event occurred, not only were there assurances from the government that the rebels would never breech the security of the city, but we were told that there were also "pre-emptive strikes" against them. Perhaps to allay the fears of the populace, the government was either guilty of horrendous complacency or irrationally misguided propaganda. Their strategy was to downplay the "size, strength, and character of the attacking forces." Unfortunately, this strategy aggravated an already precarious situation. Like the morning of 25 May 1997, we were woken up by the sound of gunfire. To many of us, it was incredible that after all the propaganda hype of government, the events of 25 May were being replicated, and by the very same people. This time they came under the guise of our country's army, but the composition was the same: the rebels and our so-called soldiers. This time round, they surrounded themselves with conscripted unarmed civilians, using them as "human shields" to breach the defences of the city which were meagre to say the least. Their strategy was not even different from the last time. They came and, as on the previous occasion, broke into the prison and released all the prisoners, many of whom were convicted of treason charges—those who served and /or aided the junta during the military interregnum.

During the previous experience of nine months of junta misrule, it was like hell in the entire country. This time, junta vengeance on the capital lasted for a shorter period, but the experience was worse than the events of the 25 May coup. Unconfirmed reports had it that for the period that the rebels were in the city, they cold-bloodedly murdered between 4,000 and 5,000 people in the city alone. Almost all of those murdered died in the most gruesome and painful circumstances. The methods used were either by gunshot, by burning, or by machete. Did the perpetrators experience any sorrow for their crimes? No. According to the TRC, the sobels did not even understand the gravity of the abuses they committed against us. In fact, stories abound about the cold-bloodedness of their acts. Take for example cases in which the rebels demanded money from people as a guarantee for sparing their houses. After payment was made by poor homeowners or tenants, the rebels would gleefully burn down the house. There were cases in which people begged for their houses not to be burned but were instantly shot because they pleaded with the rebels to spare their homes. Imagine! Many of these properties were legacies built many years ago. Many also were the culmination of people's lifetime savings. All just went up in flames. It is extremely sad to think that many of these perpetrators were little boys and girls who were still wet behind their ears. What a tragedy!

After these catastrophic and catatonic events, will Sierra Leone ever be the same again? So much housing, educational, and health infrastructure destroyed; business premises vandalised, all their equipment destroyed. Of course, Sierra Leone has come a long way since independence, and the environment keeps changing. Change can be better or worse; it can also be beneficial or unprofitable. In my country, there have been changes. These changes might have benefited a few individuals in the short run, but on the whole, one is apt to conclude that change in our country has only impoverished and degraded the majority of its people. In spite of all this, our politicians and businessmen continue their rape and plunder all in the furtherance of private capitalism, evermore leaving the nation more impoverished.

Briefly, our country happily attained self-rule in 1961 when we apparently shed the yoke of colonial rule, but since then, what do we have to show for it? No street lighting, a city of darkness where we cannot even solve our energy problem, but we are not even resource poor, landlocked, or bounded by a wide expanse of ocean, yet we are classed as least developed. Now that the UN system has come up with a holistic classification of development, the Human Development Index (HDI), for a while now, our country has languished at the bottom; upstanding and sound-thinking countrymen should weep for the parlous state of this once peaceful and beautiful country.

After so many years of independence, what development strides can we boast of? Mass illiteracy, proliferation of "pan-bodies," defacing of the city centre, congestion of street traders in the heart of the city, converting public places for private domestic use, for cooking, laundering, and washing of pots and pans. Mountains of rubbish, clogged drains, massive deforestation, desecration of sacred places, a violently carefree/careless attitude among the young, and a rapacious propensity among the old. Those in authority are not ignorant of these goings-on, but they do not know any better, are powerless to act, or are party to this destructive mentality.

Taking this scenario into account, many may be tempted to advance the rebels' cause. However, events have demonstrated adequately that they had neither a legitimate cause nor an agenda. Governance in Sierra Leone has been poor and there were many grievances, but the atrocities committed against the innocent populace was not the way to address or solve these challenges. What cause would a man who kills only to be noticed have, as colonel Maskita announced over the airwaves? The sobels proved their inability to govern when they arrogated power to themselves in 1997.

For the nine months that they enforced a military interregnum, not only did they plunder the country's treasury and resources, but also they killed all those who were not in support of them. It is doubtful whether the rebels themselves knew what they wanted. Even if they knew, the information that is now emerging points to the fact that there was definitely non-convergence between the bosses and the foot soldiers. Those who plundered and maimed were being used as tools to further the selfish ends of a few unscrupulous criminal elements that stood to profit considerably from this chaos. But those who did the actual fighting were so naive, ignorant, and pumped full of drugs (cocaine), which during the invasion they seemed to have in abundance, they wilfully and gleefully destroyed themselves and their own country.

From the near-west end of the city, on to the extreme east or the outskirts of the capital, the rebels, within the time that they were allowed free reign, wreaked untold and incomprehensible vengeance on the city's populace. Without any compunction or remorse, they killed, burnt, raped, and looted. Their actions were so indiscriminate that the people of the city were acutely traumatised.

On that fateful day, the first inclination I had that something was terribly amiss was from telephone calls made to us by extremely concerned friends seeking to know the reason for the gunshots around the west end of the city where the central prison is located. Though I pleaded ignorance, I became concerned and in turn tried to ascertain the truth of what was happening. Shortly after, I saw very unkempt and poorly dressed men carrying poly-thene bags passing by, singing songs of victory. Then I said to myself that this was May 1997 all over again.

On reaching this conclusion, I tuned my radio to a local FM station and, lo and behold, the civilian population was informed that some rebel elements had invaded the city and was advised to stay indoors until the problem was taken care of. Shortly after, another friend telephoned to inform me that the rebel commander had made an announcement from another local radio station, stating that the lawful government had been overthrown again by the rebels. The rebel commander then gave an indication of all the areas they were in control of, stating that he was speaking from the State House, the office of the president.

At that material point in time, one was overcome by a feeling of gross de-spair. After what happened in May 1997, these occurrences were extremely difficult to comprehend, and that was just the beginning of another period of disillusionment for Sierra Leoneans.

While being informed by government propaganda that the rebels would soon be chased out of the city, the civilian population to the central and east of the city was encouraged to keep up their spirit. But as time went on, we came to learn that the ECOMOG force on which we pinned our hopes had made a tactical withdrawal from the east of town where the rebels penetrated. The official reason was that the rebels, with their usual disregard for life, used innocent civilians as human shields to penetrate the ECOMOG defences. That the rebels used unconventional tactics to penetrate government defences was partly true, but in all likelihood, the government was economical with the truth. As is recorded in the TRC report, many civilians, believing government propaganda, met an untimely death because they did not take certain precautions they would normally have taken if it were not for the information broadcast by the government radio station. From the sixth of January until well into March, the civilian population from Brookfields to the west of the city, unto Waterloo, to the extreme east, witnessed apocalypse. One catholic priest who was abducted by the rebels, on his release, described the capital as the city of Armageddon.

Did Sierra Leoneans think that the acts of the rebels during and after the coup d'état of 25 May 1997 were atrocious? Well, the acts following the invasion of the city were indescribable; the carnage was too much and difficult to bear. How could the wilful burning down of houses with the owners or occupiers inside be explained, plus the raping of old women, the slaughter of entire families, and maiming of and abduction of children? Of course, this was the motto of the rebels in 1997 until they were kicked out by the ECOMOG; then they were not given the time to regroup so they had to retreat in haste to save themselves. What they achieved then was unplanned and haphazard. This time round, they had the time to vent their evil and despicable designs on innocent people. Yes, it might be true that the government was incompetent in the way and manner they administered governance, including the military, on resumption of democratic rule in 1998, but the acts of the SLA cannot be excused.

Although the invasion occurred on 6 January, the rebels or many of them were in the city long before that date. Not only were they in the city, but they were able to move heavy weaponry into the city. How was that possible with the ECOMOG headquarters in the city, and right under the nose of all of us citizens in the city? In the TRC report, it is stated that "the government and ECOMOG" had received intelligence reports of RUF/AFRC collaborators filtering into Freetown, in advance of the invasion that ranged from reconnaissance to hoarding of arms and ammunition. It cannot be said we all were ignorant, or were that dumb, not to have noticed unusual movements or strange faces around our locality. But as it turned out, the degree of collaboration among the civil populace with the rebels was quite high, even to the detriment of some of the collaborators. It became a case in which the monster got out of control once it was given its head.

Apparently, the rebels were countrymen. Evidently, they even had relatives in the city. So many of them were given safe havens during the planning stages of the invasion; they ate and slept with their relatives who could not have claimed ignorance of their evil intent. Perhaps, they reasoned, that they were not in support of this particular government even though they had the people's mandate. Also, somewhere down the road, a long time ago, the rebels themselves including their leaders lost sight of whatever cause they were fighting for. So many of us were misguided individuals and parochial in our thinking. Who in his or her rightful mind would have held any brief for the rebel movement, let alone supported it after the experience of over ten years of carnage and the events following the military interregnum between May 1997 and February 1998? No, but with us, the reasoning was, we were of the same tribe, we came from the same area, and he or she was my relative so I must give him or her unstinted support. From then on, like the rebels themselves, they were no longer Homo sapiens but only robots programmed to give irrational support no matter if this support would result in crimes against humanity. This attitude will be with us for a long time, especially considering our low levels of political, social, and economic enlightenment.

However, happen it did, and we countrymen were the worst for it. Let's not talk about the dead; they have gone to the great beyond, a well-travelled road, but one in which none of us has any experience of. Not even second hand. Thousands of people were made homeless and were now sleeping rough or in makeshift camps. In our midst, there are countless men, women, and children with hacked-off limbs.

Considering that we live in a country where people are so poor, salaries are so low, and the bulk of the people are unemployed, where one could not even secure a mortgage to build a house, how could one replace such assets, many of which were legacies bequeathed to children and relatives? Yet so many platforms were calling for amnesty, blanket amnesty, power sharing, even rewarding the rebels financially so that they would have emigrated. But what I never heard in all these highfaluting discussions was who would pay for this carnage, who was going to compensate those who had lost the breadwinners in their families, or who was going to build these houses or replace these lost assets. But perhaps we should not be perplexed at all, as after the city's invasion, suddenly the newspapers and many people started clamouring for peace at any cost. No matter what kind of solution came out at the end, the question was "Who will pay for all the carnage, all the destruction and the amputations?" Definitely not the government, who in the final analysis would broker any peace, or the donor community, which shied away from contributing to permanent shelter—not in Africa anyway. But who will blame them, or why blame them for that matter? They could not be pumping hard-earned taxpayers' money into our country, which is potentially richer than most, only to see their hard-earned financial resources frittered away by irresponsible and corrupt officials (rebels).

After the catastrophic events of 1997, there was still a lot of goodwill and sympathy in the international community for the people of our country. Following this, the road to peace and the rebuilding of the shattered economy and highly traumatised people was fervently pursued by sympathisers and nationals alike. A lot of resources were invested by the donor community, especially, the British and the Americans, and we should not underrate the Nigerians who supported us both in human and financial resources, perhaps more than any other country, and they have continued to support their African brothers.

In the early days of the invasion, our countrymen believed the rebels' claim that they were tired of fighting and had come out of the bush because they wanted peace. From experience, there were those who were wary, but encouraged by the gun to come out and dance for peace. Many people, young and old, both women and men, in fear of retribution went out to "jubilate" with the rebels. In the final days, did this save them? Unequivocally, no! Every civilian was enemy to the rebels, and many were slaughtered like sheep.

Long before the carnage started, the rebels had embarked on their course of destruction. There was jubilation among those behind rebel lines when the president went on the radio to announce the release of the rebel leader Foday Sankoh, contingent on the cessation of hostilities on all sides of the conflict. Did the rebels accept? No. Instead, the notorious Maskita, their field commander, rejected the proposition advanced by the government and people of our country and thereby went on to order his fighters to destroy the city. Then, the rebels went on a killing and burning spree.

Although the rebels were pushed out of the city, sadly, they laid waste to entire communities in Kissy, Wellington, Calabar town, Waterloo, and beyond. Despicably, on their retreat, they abducted over two thousand young children, especially girls, many of whom were more enlightened than their abductors and who were nurtured to live and behave like human beings, not like beasts in the jungle.

Soon after the rebel carnage of January 1999 which engulfed the entire country, the talk was we had suffered enough and wanted peace. In this context, peace at any cost. Unfortunately, after so many years, we have peace but are still counting the cost. Nonetheless, we must take heart and thank the good Lord. The DRC cannot make up their minds whether they have peace or are still in the throes of a rebel war. Somalia is on a path of self-destruction.

This clamour for peace started a train in which the international community brought pressure to bear on the government of this "banana republic" to talk peace with the rebels. This happened at a time when the rich diamond fields and fertile pasturelands were in the hands of the sobels. Our government, like the sheep they were, went ahead to beg for peace from the high and mighty corporal. Even when the civil society movement stood up against bringing the sobels into government, our lacklustre government's tune changed from one that was a government of national unity to that of a government of inclusion. Not being a legal luminary myself, only the revered attorney-general could differentiate between the two. The Lome Peace Accord that was signed in July 1999 is now history, but its effects on the poor, trampled, and traumatised people are still heavy on our shoulders.

CHAPTER 10

AFTER THE LOME PEACE ACCORD

Foday Sankoh, RUF leader with some of his top commandos.

Although a peace agreement was signed in Lome, this sought-after peace continued to be elusive. Like so many other times, the sobels could not be trusted. They reneged in Abidjan, so also did they in Conakry. Why or how on earth could we have trusted them? As the saying goes, "A leopard never changes its spots." But alas, our leaders were that gullible. The sobels were in control of the diamond areas; who in their right mind would have given up such wealth at the stroke of a pen? After several years of civil strife, there seemed to be a fragile peace, guaranteed by external stakeholders, notably by the international community. When the peace came, it was sudden and unexpected but welcomed by all and sundry. Like the Trojans, we were flabbergasted by war. However, between the signing of Lome and the dramatic events of 2002 that led to the cessation of hostilities, there was no peace. The sobels were still in control of the richly productive areas. For countrymen, the whole idea of diplomacy was turned on its head. In our case, when there was no trust, and previous accords had been broken, the next option was the diplomatic option. If that had not succeeded, the other option would have been more diplomacy! Keep on talking to the so-bels until they had extracted all the wealth in the country, continued with their abuse of our human rights, raping our women and terrorising our villages. Then the diplomatic option would have succeeded. Only where would we be? Apparently, under the yoke of the sobels. And for this, we would have had no one to thank but our so-called government under the erstwhile leadership of the much-revered man of peace, highly religious and of *impeccable credentials!* Unfortunately, for us downtrodden and poor countrymen, we did not have a statesman of stature. We only had Johnny Paul. With him, we would have co-existed with Sankoh and his cohorts as long as nobody rocked the boat. Our president could not mobilise or animate his people to stand up against the riff-raff Sankoh, Maskita, and their ilk. But then our country is not an island. We must not forget that the rogue and rebel godfather Charles Taylor was our neighbour.

In keeping with the peace agreement, as agreements went, some of the clauses were implemented and lo and behold, the sobels were all over us. Sankoh was given the portfolio of commissioner for strategic resources, which included all our mineral wealth and more. In like manner, we had ministers from the rogue movement, the sobels. Not that it was novel to them; after all, did not Johnny Paul, our former head of state, bring the sobels into government? But alas, that was an illegitimate regime and poor Johnny Paul did not know it.

So Sankoh was legitimised by our man of peace and ranked alongside the vice president. Nobody bothered to gauge the feelings of Sierra Leoneans. How did it feel to sit in a meeting with a monster? How could one have imagined Foday Sankoh, sitting down in cabinet, making policy decisions and the like? This was the hard reality of life in the republic of Sierra Leone. With all the noise and fanfare, how did the RUF utilise this legitimacy and taste of power that was conferred upon them by an already weak and totally inept government?

Considering what had gone before, all the heinous crimes committed against a docile and tame people, a rational being would have embraced the opportunity to atone for past misdeeds and try to replace the things that they had destroyed. That is, those things that could be replaced; many of the things that they had destroyed were lost forever. We should not fool ourselves. Priceless things can never be replaced. Indeed, the sad thing was how many of us realised this truth? We have been plodding on in our little backyard as if nothing had happened. Opportunities were created, opportunistic moments were given us, but we still trampled our land like zombies, being led by the same group of uninspired generals, up with their old tricks of destruction and rape, always pointing fingers at corruption but doing nothing about it. Did we not read in the papers and are still reading about millions going missing, public offices being abused by petty-minded people, unholy deals being concluded by government officials? But did anything happen? Of course, yes. The Anti-Corruption Commission suddenly reared its head. Don't we have laws that embrace all of these? Somebody must be fooling somebody. Thank God, we are not all fools. Nevertheless, where did this leave our poor and impoverished nation? We were just drifting by the whims and caprices of our benefactors, the donor community. You could not fault them. They do not have half as much of the resources that we have, yet we unashamedly go begging, cap in hand. We have made our country in such a way that pride and integrity were no longer virtues to strive for and emulate. We sold that a long time ago.

All this talk about the Athens of West Africa must be a sham; something unholy and unpleasant must have been festering all this time. People are apt to blame our ills on the past APC government, specifically the leader, Siaka Stevens. Much as that may be true, the blame goes way beyond that. Siaka Stevens and the APC government were what the populace made them to be. Theirs was only a reflection of our transgressions. Siaka Stevens is no longer with us, the APC government as we used to know it was not in power, but the rut has still not departed; in fact, the edifice was so rotten that it seemed to be crumbling.

Enough, the sobel was now part and parcel of government. The war was started to get rid of this cankerworm in our society. *Be happy, you hapless countrymen. Salvation is at hand.* Yes, that was how simplistic our minds were. We could neither reflect nor fathom the devices of evil. There was much talk about forgiveness but scarcely any on remorse and repentance. So the RUF in their evil minds did not think they had wronged this nation. In fact, Sierra Leoneans used to listen to all of their spokesmen, leaders, and pseudo leaders spouting ideological nonsense about the liberation struggle from corrupt and polluted leaders and such trash. All the time though, they were lining their pockets from illegal diamond mining as they skilfully occupied the wealthiest areas of the country. How much of their ill-gotten gains were declared to customs? How much was officially reported? We even heard that they were doing business with the Al-Qaeda terrorist group of Osama bin Laden. Yet through the influence of the international community, including the United Nations and the United States, which had declared war on terrorism, the sobel was brought into the fold. Something must be incomprehensible here as the very United States, after 11 September, had taken some belated actions against terrorist groups, including the sobels. How did this ragtag group led by the dastardly Saybanah fare in our government of inclusion? Whatever that meant.

Sankoh was scarcely on his cabinet seat when he started showing his true colours. He refused to attend cabinet meetings or other official functions, sent contrary signals to his commanders in the field, sold our mineral resources to international rogues like himself, and prepared to subvert the government and seize the reins of power forcefully by riding roughshod over the very people that he originally set out to liberate.

Yes, Sankoh did not attend meetings because he was a law unto himself, but nobody, not even the president, had the guts to rein him in. Really, it was a great folly to bring the sobels into the realm, not even as a price for peace. Many people, flabbergasted by the war, including highly placed government functionaries, were under the misconception that this would lead to lasting peace. In truth, they did not understand the dynamics of this movement. Even if they were in control of the entire government of Sierra Leone, there might have been no war, but there would have been complete and utter chaos, and they would have kept on doing what they were good at: abusing human rights. Let us not make any mistakes about that. That was the psyche of the rebel movement in our country. Taking a closer look at their outfit, there was no ideology; what they propagated was contradictory and incomprehensible. In plain language, Sankoh and his gang were just propelled by hate and greed. Contrary to popular belief, even the hate was unjustified; the end in this case did not justify the means. They could not have satisfied these tendencies unless they were in control of the country's resources and to achieve that they had to go on a killing, maiming, and burning spree of innocent civilians, their assets, and their villages. By instilling this mass fear, they ought to have succeeded. Pure Machiavellian!

In all of this, after beating death row, Sankoh would have thought he was invincible, but like others before him, he was not. He was not a student of history but guerrilla warfare. He passed through the Gaddafi academy of terrorism in Libya, after which, according to gathered intelligence, he went on a killing spree, annihilating the elite of the movement, hijacked it, and turned it into a killing machine. He might have been taught about Saloth Sar, popularly known as Pol Pot in Cambodia. Although not on the same scale, what happened in our country must have been similar to what happened in Cambodia; this place was the killing fields also, especially the events of December 1998/January 1999. What was the fate of Pol Pot? He evaded justice for a while, but his past finally caught up with him. In our case here, our "brothers," the rebels who were being disarmed, were clamouring for the release of their leader, Sankoh, who was under lock and key for human rights violation. And all our attorney-general could retort was that it was not in our government's hands but the international community! That was preposterous! Sankoh committed crimes against humanity because he violated the human rights of native countrymen and not the international community. Our government too had the right to bring charges against him. But the government's stand was understandable. That was how they had survived up till now by dodging issues and waiting for a push from the international community.

For a sovereign state, even our security was not in our hands but in UNAMSIL's, whose mandate was not to confront the rebels but to maintain the peace, meaning the existing status quo at a cost. Iraqis demanded strongly that Saddam Hussein should be handed over to them—the very people he abused, mauled, and mutilated. Why did the AG become so timid that he passed the buck? But the international community was happy, so were the sobels; in this climate, they could pursue their illegal agenda of enriching their pockets and terrorising the civil populace, thereby gaining international acclaim by their own reckoning and some other misguided minds. How else could the BBC have broadcast a sketch of that notorious Maskita in the guise of fame? Those of us who heard that eulogy were appalled but rightly concluded that it portrayed the notoriety of the sobel as epitomised by the Maskita colonel. The Maskita colonel might not be physically present with us, but all that he stood for was abhorrent and anathema. We had rogues like Issa Sesay and Gibril Massaquoi to be dealt with. Really, whatever happened to our once glorious country?

In spite of all this, Foday Sankoh was made a VIP, but he thought he should have been made a VVIP and given the rank of vice president. And in fact, he behaved and lived like one, making unilateral decisions, even those that involved state matters. He was not even president, but he was behaving like a dictator of the worst kind, all in the name of the liberation struggle. Sankoh and the sobels wanted indeed to liberate the people of Sierra Leone, not from tyranny or parochialism but from their wealth, property, and orderly lives, acts in which they succeeded to a large extent. For their success, they became stakeholders and were given political recognition. According to them, they had transformed themselves into a political party, but they still had their guns and were reluctant to disarm. They wanted to establish their party, but unlike other parties, they expected the government and the international community to give them everything gratis. Of course, they vanquished everything that was sacred in our society, so why not make them absolute monarchs so that they could complete the job they started in March 1991? In his short term in office, Sankoh had mortgaged the country's resources to other rogues like himself, a task he was going to complete on his ascendancy as president of the Republic of Jungle Land. Thank God, that did not happen. Many sane-thinking countrymen would have been slaughtered like Pol Pot did to the Cambodians, all in the name of the revolution.

CHAPTER 11

THE FALL OF FODAY SANKOH

By the start of the new millennium, there was general scepticism about the sincerity of the RUF and civil society was still not comfortable with having them in government. The playing field was indeed not level and our benevolent government did not even see that. After Lome, the direction of authority and general traffic was one way. Suddenly, the city was awash with "the brothers" bragging about their past misdeeds, and who dared go against them? That was their democratic right (i.e., freedom of movement, speech, and association). For their own part, the sobels refused to accept the authority of the government in rebel-held areas. But worse still, no rational individual was allowed to access those areas, even local inhabitants who were domiciled in those localities. By the end of 1998, the sobels were really in control of a large swathe of the country, including the rich diamondiferous zone, evidenced by testimonies in the TRC report. People's houses and property were confiscated and occupied by the sobels. This was in continuation with wealth redistribution as started by the illegal military junta of Johnny Paul. Fancy after labouring for years to put a roof over your head, a stranger/rebel came and confiscated your property because he wanted to liberate you from corruption, tyranny, and dishonest and unscrupulous politicians.

Feeling invincible—after all, they were in control of the greater and most productive areas of the country—they had the backing of the real leader,

Charles Taylor, and the peacekeepers were just toothless bulldogs. They decided it was time to make their grand play and seize the reins of government. Skirmishes erupted in the northern axis, especially for control of the town that was the gateway to and from the provinces. After claims and counter claims, fighting even among pro-government forces, this town and its environs finally fell to the sobels. The government by then had retrained part of the military, which apparently took the fight to the rebels. But as usual, they were not fighting for a cause but for themselves. Thus, they became disgruntled when promotions were made and their names were not included.

In pursuit of their grand plan, the UNAMSIL peacekeeping force stationed in the east, specifically in the productive areas, was encircled and placed under siege. Government had to negotiate with the rebels even to get their food rations to them. More seriously though, a contingent of over five hundred UNAMSIL peacekeepers was seized with their weapons, including some heavy weaponry, and all by mere boys, and held hostage. Poor UNAMSIL. Who can blame them? Even with their so-called superior firepower, they were mesmerised by a ragtag rebel force consisting mainly of teenage boys and girls. But again, stricken countrymen should not forget that these peacekeepers were only here to keep the peace and their mandate did not allow them to fight. Was the United Nations so blind that it could not have foreseen the situation into which it was sending a peacekeeping force? In any event, it was fortuitous for us that the British came in with a more robust mandate to compensate for the impotence of the UN force. A more robust mandate would have done the trick; this was only realised on hindsight, but at what cost?

The British were unilateral, so decision-making was not too difficult. With the United Nations, decision-making was multilateral with so many divergent views pulling one way or the other. But again, might it not have been that the United Nations was distracted by other agendas, private they may have been, but the consequences did not alter. After all, the top military man in UNAMSIL did accuse some of their top brass of engaging in the extraction business for which cause he was replaced by informed wisdom. Be that as it was, this ragtag rebel movement backed by their godfather

Charles Taylor held UNAMSIL ransom and made so many demands on government. The entire situation was so farcical, considering the fact that the sobels up to that time were part of the government, but their actions showed otherwise.

All this was a prelude to the grand plan of Poppay, Foday Sankoh. After all, it is documented that Sankoh signed the peace accord not because he wanted peace or was tired of fighting but because, according to him, he signed "to relieve international pressure on the RUF." He also ordered his men to continue fighting. That was to have come to fruition on 8 May, which was a Monday. In fact, things started happening the previous day as, according to UNAMSIL, the rebels were less than twenty miles from the city, the capital. The UN spokesman in a panic made that announcement and sent the entire western area into catatonic shock. Where the rebels were said to have reached was an area where one of the UNAMSIL battalions had bivouacked. By inference, that announcement could only portray that their positions had been breached by the rebels. Visions of May 1997 and January 1999 must have been evoked. The result was the city became deserted and tension was in the air, caused by that single announcement by the UN spokesman. But again, we should have understood their panic; their mandate, which was not robust enough, tied their hands behind their backs. How could you have carried so much weaponry, some very heavy, if you did not intend to use them? The answer, painful as it may have been, was that they brought them to be used by the rebels against innocent civilians. If this was not the case, then there was a serious flaw in the decision-making process at the United Nations.

The long and short of it was these weapons were captured by the sobels and turned against the people on that fateful Monday in May 2000. On that day, it was alleged that Foday Sankoh was going to be proclaimed president. Providence as always took a hand in the affairs of this country. That was the day that civil society unknowingly decided to march against this monster. March to his sumptuous residence they did, to let the whole world know that Sierra Leoneans were fed up with the posturing of the sobels and that we wanted peace. As it turned out then, we did not get this peace that we had long been craving for but bloodshed, as once again innocent civilians were massacred by the beast and his brood of followers. What started as a peaceful demonstration turned to murder as over twenty innocent lives were cut down in their prime.

The crowning folly of all this was that UNAMSIL was there with tanks, apparently guarding the pseudo Excellency's residence. But as it turned out, it looked like they were there to protect Foday Sankoh, as in the heat of the moment with all these tanks and peacekeepers, even after committing such atrocities, he was able to escape. Indeed, it appeared to many as if the peacekeepers used diversionary tactics for the monster to escape. Many people were of the opinion that when one of the tanks guarding the premises left the scene of the crime, it was taking Sankoh away to save him from the wrath of the crowd. Lo and behold, when the situation had settled down a bit, the presence or no presence of Foday Sankoh became a mystery. Some were of the opinion that he was in the custody of UNAMSIL, which claimed ignorance of his whereabouts. But, of course, we thought this was a diplomatic ploy to stabilise the situation. But this did not turn out to be so: he was at large. Why shouldn't he be? He was a countryman free to move about as in all this, no official charges were preferred against him—not by the government at any rate. Who would have blamed them? They did it before. He was even sentenced to death, but all in the guise of peace he was given a presidential pardon to continue doing what he knew best: butchering innocent women and children. He had been doing that all along when he started the war, perhaps even before then as he slaughtered the elite in the rebel movement.

Foday Sankoh escaped, but government was able to gain unhindered access to his fortress. And what did they find? Astoundingly, there was incriminating evidence galore implicating even some members of parliament and foreigners as so-called investors and arms and ammunition, even though the residence was under constant surveillance by the UNAMSIL. What was the upshot to all this?

It was a great find for the government, and true to form, they wasted no time in calling a press conference to reveal the treasures that were discovered in Vice President Sankoh's residence. Much propaganda was made about this treasure trove, but the disclosure as to the find was preciously scanty. In their predetermined mind-set, the government went as silent as night. Nothing more was heard and for those things that were found, no action was taken. This was a government of abdication; they abdicated the seat of government in 1997 during the military junta of the sobels and on returning in March 1998 abdicated their responsibility to govern. Many countrymen felt, and rightly so, their government failed to protect them; they condoned corruption, never mind the establishment of an anti-corruption commission, and failed to heed the call of civil society.

The government became impotent, our legislators became lukewarm, while UNAMSIL became powerless. But the British came in quite heavily. They were able to stabilise the situation, freed the encircled peacekeepers in Kailahun, and even cleared the Westside boys from a strategic location in the western area, all in the blinking of an eye. Neither the UNAMSIL nor the government was able to accomplish this feat. In fact, UNAMSIL went on an operation seemingly to clear the Westside boys from their location where they were a threat to security and causing all manner of untold criminal acts against the people. In ecstatic mood, UNAMSIL as usual announced the successful completion of their mission that we thought was to rid us of the Westside boys' menace. However, what they succeeded in doing was to drive them from the roadside where they usually mounted their checkpoints into the bush where they committed more criminal liaisons. But thanks to the British contingent and the abject stupidity of the West Side Boys, they were cut down to size by a well-disciplined force and cleared from their stronghold. When that happened, we really could not understand why these boys were left to their own mischief for so long. Accordingly, the usual rumours went round the mill.

Once the international community's interest became focused upon our country's problem, things suddenly started to move. What became topical in various circles was this: did the world at large have to wait until UN peacekeepers were kidnapped before acknowledging the plight that we as Sierra Leoneans had been going through for several years in the hands of the sobels before being involved? Or were the lives of the five hundred or so peacekeepers abducted more important than other Sierra Leoneans behind rebel lines? Becoming involved they did.

First, Charles Taylor, who stridently denied having any links with the sobels, agreed to talk them into releasing the peacekeepers, which he did. But even though they were being held in Sierra Leone, they had to be released via Liberia; perhaps proof enough that he was heavily involved with the sobels. Once that assertion was made, although he continued to protest his innocence, the international community started moving against him.

Once this action commenced, certain damning facts were revealed, like the involvement of other individuals within and without the sub-region in the conflict. The TRC report adequately chronicles the involvement of external players and their impact on the conflict: the smuggling of diamonds into Liberia and the proceeds subsequently used for the purchasing of arms destined for the sobels through Burkina Faso, then onwards to Liberia, from whence they were smuggled into the rebel strongholds in Sierra Leone. There was also the forceful recruitment of refugees into the rebel movement. All these crimes were squarely laid at the doorstep of Charles Taylor. Of course, he continued to deny vehemently. Even when accused by the British and the Americans, he harangued about producing the proof of these allegations, which of course they did. The result was specific sanctions levied by the UN Security Council against him. The actions, unfortunately, did not produce the desired effect. If one was to study his psyche, one would conclude that his was a destabilising influence through and through that can only thrive when there was a complete breakdown of an organised system. Hence, Liberia's conflict has been over for some time, but what did the despotic Taylor do to rebuild the country for which he was the elected president? All he did was to enrich himself and impoverish an already traumatised nation. He could not even conceive of a plan to bring his country to where it was before he pulverised it, let alone take it forward into the twenty-first century.

In the mould that he was cast, he made the mistake of trying to do to his other neighbour Guinea what he succeeded in doing in our country. Similar to our country, Guinea has diamonds. Perhaps he thought he could reap some benefits there. Unfortunately for him, that country was unlike Sierra Leone. Any fool could have told him that. But of course, being the maniac that he was, his senses were atrophied by greed and power. He was pounded from all sides; he of course had to turn to his former sobel colleagues for help to stem the tide. That failed woefully as again the sobels were mauled, battered, and slaughtered like cannon fodder. Therein lay the freeing of our country from the grips of the sobel. In fact, it became so hot for them in the north of the country where they had been a law unto themselves that they had to literally beg UNAMSIL to deploy, which they had resisted before.

Because of the absence of civil authority in the greater part of the north and the presence of the sobel, no sane individual or organisation was prepared to do any kind of work whatsoever in those areas at the time, even taking humanitarian relief to the beleaguered population of the north. It was common knowledge that one did so at his or her own risk. The few attempts that were made to engage the sobel in some form of interaction ended in disaster. Notwithstanding this common knowledge to all and sundry, there were some politicians who were castigating the government for apparently neglecting that area. Those who had woefully failed to win the support of their constituents jumped on the bandwagon of sectionalism to further their own selfish ends even in the face of such horrendous crisis that was confronting the country. After all we went through, there was no uniting banner under which we could stand as Sierra Leoneans. Only the president would have gone public stating that there was no tribalism in the country; he was definitely out of touch with reality.

Circumstances forced the sobels to disarm in the north, but the rich diamond and agricultural areas of Kono, Tongo field in the Kenema district and Kailahun respectively, were intransigent. After several meetings and agreements, there were always excuses to stall the process. Such reasons like the freeing of jailed sobel personnel, the non-payment of transitional subsistence allowance (TSA), the provision of office space and houses for the sobel party, and the provision of security were usually adduced. The government, being what it was, and the UNAMSIL, based on the less robust mandate, trod carefully. In truth, the sobels were calling the shots.

Consequently, the end date for the disarmament process was put back so many times that we, the ordinary people, wondered whether the process was ever going to end.

End it did. On 18 January 2002, Kabbah declared the war was over at a ceremony held at the Lungi Airport.

Did we all breathe a sigh of relief? After so long and with so many disappointments and broken promises on the way, could we be comfortable with the current status quo? The war was now over, but we were still talking about consolidating the peace. There also was and still is talk about poverty reduction and good governance. To give Kabbah his due, local government proscribed for over thirty years by the APC government was re-established.

A new order was supposed to have been heralded by the cessation of hostilities, but many were sceptical and also cynical. Who would blame the sceptics or the cynics? The expectants we can blame because they were not living in this world. If we did not make a U-turn in 1998 when constitutional rule was restored after so much suffering, were we going to change now that we expected things to be better? Sierra Leoneans have a very porous memory. Soon we will even forget about the war and the untold suffering it brought down upon us. But that should be a good sign as we are being reminded to forgive and forget.

Once again, our country did prove that it was unique. In the midst of turmoil and continuing instability, the war period came to a dramatic and abrupt end. Not perhaps due to the statesmanship of our leaders but to the pulverisation of the sobels by outside forces, notably the neighbours and the British; the annihilation of large contingent of their troops drilled some sense into them, together with the incarceration of their leader after the 8 May debacle. This act perhaps demystified the Poppay cult of Saybanaism.

This peace that came suddenly brought some ray of hope to many of us, although there was some wariness in many hearts as the general elections had not yet been held. Considering where we were coming from and the prevailing conditions at the time, there was a general sense of foreboding at the forthcoming general elections. But the elections have come and gone, held in a peaceful atmosphere. The Palm Tree led by the intrepid Tejan Kabbah won another five-year term with the mandate to bring about para-digmical change, but did they? A few years down the line, we are grappling with food security and poverty reduction.

The disarmament and demobilisation exercise was complete and the presi-dent himself on that fateful day in January declared that peace had finally come to Sierra Leone. Bravo! He was good at making pronouncements but not so good at following them up to the copy or spirit of the letter.

Also, he might be good at keeping up appearances. In 1996, country-men had such high hopes in the new dispensation, especially coming from a military dictatorship mired in a seemingly never-ending conflict. Unfortunately, nothing appeared to have changed; the sufferings the na-tion experienced did not galvanize our resolve. Notwithstanding, all was not lost. In resisting the military junta, Sierra Leoneans had earned the respect of the international community. And so our man of peace was able to establish a government in exile, and at that time, countrymen took heart. Dr Julius Spencer, Mr Allie Bangurah, and Ms Hannah Fullah in their Radio Freedom broadcasts and a host of many others gave hope to many of us who stayed behind, noting that it was also not easy for many of those who left and sought refuge elsewhere. This was a time when life was as cheap as listening to FM 98.1. If you were caught listening to that station, the sentence was summary execution by the sobels or their sym-pathisers. In those troubled days, nobody, but nobody, thought that the day of reckoning would come. Now they are here, the special court for crimes against humanity and the Truth and Reconciliation Commission (TRC) have been established. Horrendous tales have come out. In spite of all the probable reasons that were adduced for the conflict, the real reasons and those hiding behind the establishment may never be revealed.

CHAPTER 12

OLD TRICKS DIE HARD

When the sobels were given the right and opportunity to become a legitimate entity, they claimed that they were going to win the general elections. They would have thought like Charles Taylor, having destroyed the country they should have been given the opportunity to rebuild. Thank God, it did not happen; we would have witnessed another round of strife as happened with our neighbours. Throughout the war, the sobels had claimed they were fighting to topple corruption by the overthrow of corrupt governments. However, the hidden agenda was the plundering of the country's diamonds. Various testimonies in the TRC report illustrate the desperate attempts made by Foday Sankoh and his RUF foot soldiers to control the diamond areas. In many instances, proceeds of the illegal sale of diamonds were used to beef up their weapons arsenal. The conduit was through Libya, Burkina Faso, and Liberia. In a similar manner, the government of the day employed this resource, that is diamonds, to entice private security firms and mercenaries to defend and protect its interests. To exploit this rich resource, they needed power, which they held briefly in 1997/1998 but severely disrupted from 1998 to 2001.

Now that terrorism has been legitimised in Sierra Leone and the world over, they had the opportunity to form the government according to their spokesperson. It is difficult to visualise the sobels leading a resurgence of a fallen country, having lived and inculcated the ways of animals in the jungle. If they were still of the opinion that they did their compatriots a favour by liberating them of their property, their limbs, and their lives, how could they begin to conceptualise the facets of good leadership and sympathy that should be shown to the innocent people who bore the brunt of their brutality and barbarism? While many of their victims were in camps, living on sympathy and goodwill, they were haranguing the government for their transitional safety allowances to allow them resettle in their communities. But who would blame them? To secure the peace, these barbarians had to be given all the encouragement they needed. Not even the handicapped and dispossessed population was left behind. Unfortunately, these were packages brokered by the international community.

After all our travails, hopes, and expectations, we are up to our old tricks again. Over ten years of a horrendous war, over twenty-five years of economic penury brought about by massive pillage of our resources by our leaders, and endemic economic mismanagement and pervasive corruption, nothing had changed. Our leaders continued to plunder and mismanage the country. All our social and economic indicators continued to degenerate: people were dying in droves because of stress, poverty, and disease. With all good intentions, I believe, President Kabba was talking about nobody going hungry within five years. Unfortunately, this pronouncement has not been concretised. During his first presidential address to Parliament after the military interregnum, he mentioned attracting foreign direct investment as a priority. Again, during his tenure of office, this did not materialise. Considering the parlous state of the country, it will be difficult to get investors to invest in Sierra Leone. The energy sector was grossly underdeveloped, the communication system was appalling, in a country blessed with more than adequate rainfall, the majority of the people do not have access to potable water, the cities are unsanitary and grossly overcrowded with overutilised amenities, etc. Yet we had a chairman of the city council traipsing all over the place politicking instead of doing the job. But what could he have done? After all, he was not elected by the people and therefore not accountable to them but to a corrupt and incompetent government. So who cares? The country was in anarchy. The city being free, one followed his or her whims and caprices. The law, what law? The law was there to be exploited by those in authority at the expense of the downtrodden masses

One can go on and on with an unending tale of degradation and dehumanising of the masses. Come election time, the elections are going to be rigged and like in the past, the masses will be duped by promises that would never be fulfilled. Countrymen must be a pitiful lot to continue to vote for the same hopelessly worthless government. But perhaps the government cannot be called totally useless; didn't they accede to the special court? Or did they? Was this to show the world justice prevailed in our society? How interesting considering that the judicial system in the country is corrupt, widely abused and misused by those in authority. Simple and straightforward cases drag on for years because the aggrieved party does not have any political clout and financial backing or the accused is one of the "big men." To the man in the street, it would appear those in authority were blind to the idiosyncrasies of the system. But they will be, if they are the very ones that compromised it.

Like it or not, the special court is here. The president, accepting the inadequacies of our judicial system, requested the United Nations to set up a special court to try perpetrators of crimes against humanity. When individuals like the late Sam Hingha Norman, who was deputy minister of defence at the time, were indicted, there was some disaffection with the special court. Also, considering the cost, which certain quarters considered astronomical, many people were not comfortable with the proceedings, especially as only a handful of the perpetrators were arraigned before the court.

The special court was established through legislation and there was not much dissent, so there must be popular acclamation to the establishment of this court. However, there were complaints over its dealings as the arm of the court is long and not restricted to reining in only combatants and their leaders on the side of the rebels. The law, as the saying goes, has a long arm. When people fighting for the democratically elected government were brought before the courts, the shouting, criticising started with a vigour. How can the deputy minister of defence be indicted? Where does the buck stop? What about the commander of the armed forces who was no other personality than the president? Perhaps he should not be blamed; after all, in his glasshouse, he did not experience power cuts, he was supplied with water regularly, who dared tamper with his communications system, such an important personality. Traffic congestion, what did he know about traffic congestion? When he drove along, the road was cleared even hours before he would pass and he just zoomed past. All this, of course, was done in the name of security. You cannot expose the head of state to security threats. He alone was more important than the entire nation put together. Why else did we spend hours in the traffic queue just to travel a few yards, drive on very bad and poorly maintained roads. And who would believe that all owners of motor vehicles pay a fuel tax which is to be used for road maintenance? But who cared? Nobody complained. But how could one complain when you read in the daily tabloids' glowing tributes being paid to those who should get on with the job. Whether it was the national power authority, the telecommunications, the roads authority, you name it. Our daily tabloids are full of their praises.

Yes, sycophancy is one of the things killing this nation, and then there is tribalism/regionalism. Call it what you will. Is there a link between sycophancy and tribalism? Far-fetched? I do not think so, but I am sure that if one did some research, one would find a high degree of correlation between tribalism and sycophancy. The link may be blurred, and perhaps we have never given much thought to it. tribalism breeds sycophancy—the peer in the tribe who, whether he merits it or not, expects his followers to defer to him, opening doors, carrying bags and briefcases, forming a large retinue in the offices especially if the peer tribesman is a minister or a public figure, even when he has no appointments but enjoys the largesse of the public figure.

Then there is corruption. A malignant tumour that to all intent and purpose is unrelated to the issues of tribalism and sycophancy. But is it? The excuse we Sierra Leoneans advance for corruption is that we are poor, so that gives us the liberty to steal the public coffers blind and deprive the masses of valuable goods and services that are due to them. Another popular reason that politicians especially advance for dipping their hands into public coffers is the large retinue of family members and hangers-on that they have to look after. Our solution in this case is to rob Peter to pay Peter. Very convenient. This can only happen in an environment in which the law is a toothless bulldog. There is no redress in our society, and for all the talk of good governance, the old systems do prevail. How can it not prevail? The people are part of the system that will remain inanimate if not manipulated by individuals. Therefore, if in our country we carry the art or science of recycling to extremes by recycling old politicians and old hands, those who crippled the system, what should we expect? You cannot teach old dog new tricks.

When our president established the anti-corruption commission, he was acclaimed by many and the unenlightened thought that we were ready to tackle this cankerworm in our society. But this was and still remains window dressing. The international community and Britain in particular, which have morally and financially backed the resurgence of a democratic country, had insisted that we did not return to our old ways but establish good governance and tackle all the ills that brought about the civil war in our country. How better to show to the world at large that yes, we were ready, able, and willing to undertake this significant step? However, those of us in the know, or who were realistic but grudge idealism, thought otherwise. How effective was the anti-corruption commission? How frustrating had it not been for the commissioner who had brought so many cases before the authorities but without any substantive action being taken? In spite of all this, our revered Head of State had the temerity to face the world in the BBC's *Hard Talk* programme stating categorically that he was serious in tackling corruption. In fact, the interviewer, having done his homework and not as ill-informed as our head of state, made him sweat, and it was clear that he was faring very badly in the confrontation; it was clear he never did his homework properly.

Indeed, barring that everything seems to be working smoothly in the country on the surface, the general talk was that our country was a model country with resolute and a resilient people. Nonetheless, we are still wallowing in poverty. Our social and economic statistics are appalling and, when usually published, make horrendous reading.

For all the talk about good governance, workers in the apparatus for good governance are disgruntled and frustrated. Can we point to one single encouraging facet in our country or any single item of encouragement, something that gives its largely bedraggled people any hope in the foreseeable future?

CHAPTER 13

A NEW BEGINNING?

With the end of hostilities, we breathed a sigh of relief but waited with bated breath for the turning of a new leaf. These recalcitrant sobels who arrogated power to themselves unlawfully and burnt the central bank in 1997 with a view of ridding the country of corruption completely forgot or conveniently forgot about the perpetrators, the principals, so to speak, who were lauding it all over the place. Their followers or brothers who saw the "lights" of the city in 1999 had a vision of eliminating injustice and usher in a new egalitarian society; however, they used extreme means that depopulated the country to achieve their ends. Whatever the case, those in authority at the time had the opportunity to usher in good governance and put our country on the global map once more. This was a window of opportunity to build the kind of society that we had been longing for all along, including a country free from corruption, reduction of poverty, which was no longer a facet only in the rural areas but was becoming endemic in our urban setting, developing a good and desirable infrastructure and improving educational and health standards.

Accordingly, Sierra Leone was now poised for sustainable progress, politically and economically. After so much devastation and carnage, all the ingredients existed for our country to be a great nation. This was a time that with effective and good leadership, Sierra Leone could have risen from the ashes and soar like the phoenix. Again, some people would contend that all the ingredients existed save one, and that was the leadership or the commitment of all the players, Sierra Leoneans included.

I have heard people comparing our country to Singapore, making disparaging remarks about it but glowing tributes about development in Singapore. The bone of contention was that both countries became independent about the same time; Singapore very small with very scarce natural resources did extremely well. On the other hand, with all its natural endowment, our country has performed most disastrously. Having never contributed to that debate, perhaps it was time to dig in. Really, I would never compare our Sierra Leone to Singapore, but contrast it with Switzerland, a small country with scarce resource endowment but great progress in development. Our country should have been like Switzerland, considering also its natural scenic beauty. Since the human development index was not in vogue at the time of our independence, we cannot now show how much the country has dropped. One thing we cannot defend is that we had not regressed; for alas, we were carrying all the other countries as far as the human development index applied. The usual alibi was the war, but even before the war, successive governments, be it de facto or de jure, had plundered the resources at the expense of any viable and positive change. Now that the nomenclature *good governance* is the popular term, we can explain all our travails even those of the war as caused by bad governance. Bad governance caused poverty that resulted in pervasive corruption in all spheres of life—in the religious institutions as well as the state. Strangely—or should it be logically, which is not strange—people expect religious institutions to be the paragon of virtue, and why not? They are supposed to provide moral and spiritual leadership in the community. How can they? What eludes our thinking is that the very culprits in the state machinery are the very ones who undoubtedly play the lead role in these religious institutions. Nevertheless, they are in good company as history would show that in time past, those institutions laboured under misguided virtues of holiness; in some quarters, some form of depravity still lingers on. After all, we arc only human.

Since the days of structural adjustment, speeches and policy statements abound about government providing the enabling environment for private enterprise to thrive, but the public sector would focus on the things for which it had a comparative advantage, like effective and efficient social service delivery. Unfortunately, we are still wallowing in the mire; nothing has changed. In spite of some of the perpetrators being brought to book, a culture of impunity still resides in the mentality of those holding the reins of power.

It would appear the hardship years of the war did not teach us anything. Sadly, indeed, we have not learnt lessons from the war. From the least to the greatest, the most lowly to the supreme, we have returned to our bad old ways. Considering the potential wealth of the country both natural and human, how could one explain the abysmal state that she is in? Would any sane individual want to be at the helm of such a country which is covered in filth in all aspects of the word, a country whose main cities were in perpetual darkness, one in which potable water is scarce though blessed with an abundance of rain, and moreover a country whose scenic beauty is continuously being defaced by senseless land grabbers and traders? Both at the national and local levels, there is much talk of town planning, but all is just the blowing of empty air; both levels are staffed by corrupt and selfish individuals whose aims are to line their pockets with their ill-gotten wealth. We are always talking about our tourist potential, but the tourists never come; those who pose as such have other motives. It does not take them long to gravitate to the diamond rich areas, but why not? If you can pay a paltry sum for something that is not your property and reap su-per-normal profits from virtually minimal investments, why not? The very customs officers and border guards who harass the law-abiding traveller and trader for carrying simple luxuries are the very ones who turn a blind eye to our greatest plunderers and enemies of the state.

The mind boggles when one ponders on the policies of our government; perhaps like the tourists or foreigners, they themselves have ulterior motives. In their selfishness and short-sightedness, they revel in their enclaves of wealth surrounded by squalor; from the east end of the city right on to the west end, slums, squalor, and nauseating smells assault you all the way. No longer can one see an exclusively residential area in the entire western area of the country. It is now a mix of concrete palatial dwelling houses and office buildings dotted with "pan-bodies," and of course the kiosk of petty traders plying their trade even in the central business district, where certain important thorough fares have been commandeered by petty traders.

Public transport in the city is lacking, but private enterprise leaves much to be desired. Taxicabs, *poda poda* vans, and now the *okadas,* the major means of transportation in the city, are a death trap. The majority of these vehicles are not roadworthy, yet they all have or purport to have fitness certificates; this is an illustration of how our country is governed or, even after ten years of civil war, being mismanaged. The list is endless, and when the backwardness of the country is a topical agenda, the authorities hide behind the cloak of a ten-year rebel war as the excuse, but not the reason for where we find ourselves in the development spectrum.

What this country needs is a visionary but strong, committed, and determined leadership that practices the paradigm of social, cultural, and economic change. Unfortunately, we cannot boast of such in over fifty years of independence. The late Siaka Stevens had all the attributes, but his leanings were extremely skewed towards the left-hand path. It was he who pronounced, "Oosie den tie cow nar day ee go eat grass." Since then, pilfering and squandering of public funds have become profligate and legitimate. But give the Devil his due; with the old man, you knew where you were and what he was going to do. With others after him, the situation has been different. They preached morality and practised immorality, deceiving the masses with political diatribes, promises that they knew they had no intention of keeping. Who would blame them? Because of tribal or ethnic affiliations, they would be returned to office times without number. The yardstick for gaining office was not how well you performed but where you belonged and came from. The president might disagree, but he used to sit in his Eiffel Tower and was being fed by those around him who were only concerned with feathering their own nests.

With all its wealth, beautiful beaches, hills and valleys, Sierra Leone should be an idyllic place. In addition, there are abundant mineral and marine resources. Yet the country's inhabitants languish in abject poverty and squalor. Through the ages, as history has shown, we have become brutal, lazy, and complacent. Instead of being entrepreneurs and utilising our God-given wealth to better the country and its people, we are content to help foreigners rape the country. We are so small minded and bereft of that sense of tradition and rich heritage that we are prepared to sell our birthright for next to nothing, and then we start complaining about aliens railroading the people. Again, as a nation, we put all down to poverty; it has made us corrupt, lacking in discipline, ambitionless, stupid, and impotent to act on our own behalf.

The SLPP government, to say the least, has not served our nation well; those who belong will disagree but all the world knows that they are blinded by tribal or ethnic affiliations. Yes, part of the war years was during their tenure, but that window of opportunity to build our nation with the help and goodwill of the international community that was then prevalent was lost because of nonchalance, greed, and corruption. What do we have to show after eleven years of the Palm Tree? Not even palm oil, that comes from that tree. Yet in Malaysia, it is a big contributor to their economy.

Now, Sierra Leoneans seem to be more enlightened and wide-awake. During the last presidential and general election campaign, the Palm Tree government used state resources, both financial and human, to feather their nest and to trick or manipulate the people. Note that the then flag-bearer of the SLPP was interviewed on the BBC *Focus on Africa* programme about this, and he did not deny this assertion. The trite saying is "After all, this is Africa." How sad. They were still of the mind-set that countrymen were fools to be swayed by short-term gain and long-term pain, after eleven years of bad governance. Not even their flag bearer who entertained the youth, all and sundry, at his residence every morning, by dishing out stolen public funds succeeded in motivating the support of the electorate. Come the elections, they were trounced by the APC party. Bravo, countrymen! Authorised liars (politicians) cannot fool us anymore.

Another election has come and gone and one good thing that came out of it was the trouncing of the Palm Tree. Will the Sun Party be any better, or will they revert to their old tricks? Only time will tell. However, countrymen should hold their heads high as once again, like in 1967, an opposition party has won a general election in our country, a rare event in Africa.

GLOSSARY AND NOTES

Chapter 1
1. Page 4   "Devil on the Cross" was Ngugi Wa Thiong'o.
2. Page 4   SLPP: Sierra Leone People's Party (political party in Sierra Leone).
3. Page 4   APC: All People's Congress (political party in Sierra Leone).
4. Page 6   "You see soak lepet you call am puss" means "Wolf in sheep's clothing."
5. Page 6   "Pass ah die" means "Only when I am dead."
6. Page 6   "Dem say Bailor Barrie you say Davidson Nicol" means "Silver and gold are better than learning."
7. Page 7   "Oosie den tie cow nar day ee go eat grass" means "Make the most coming your way by fair means or foul."
8. Page 7   "Nar sense make book nor to book make sense" means "Better to be streetwise than bookwise."
9. Page 9   The Agony of a Nation: Abdul Karim Koroma.
10. Page 10   NPFL: National Patriotic Front of Liberia.
11. Page 12   "Agba Satani" means "Boss Satan."

Chapter 2
1. Page 14   *Sobels* refers to soldiers turned rebels.
2. Page 14   AFRC-RUF: Armed Forces Revolutionary Council-Revolutionary United Front.
3. Page 16   ECOMOG: Economic Commission of West African States Military Observer Group.

Chapter 3
1. Page 22   BBC: British Broadcasting Corporation.
2. Page 28   ECOWAS: Economic Commission of West African States.
3. Page 30   OAU: Organisation of African Unity, now the African Union (AU).
4. Page 30   EU: European Union.

Chapter 4
1. Page 36   DRC: Democratic Republic of Congo.

Chapter 5
1. Page 45   Port Loko, Masiaka and Kambia: Towns in Sierra Leone.
2. Page 46   Pam-Pams: Wooden canoes with outboard motors.
3. Page 48   NPRC: National Provisional Ruling Council.

Chapter 8
1. Page 67   DFID: Department for International Development (UK).
2. Page 67   DDR: Disarmament, Demobilisation and Reintegration.
3. Page 67   UNOMSIL: United Nations Observer Mission to Sierra Leone.
4. Page 70   NCDHR: National Commission for Democracy and Human Rights, now NCD (National Commission for Democracy).
5. Page 73   UNAMSIL: United Nations Mission to Sierra Leone, replacing UNOMSIL.

Chapter 11
1. Page 97   TSA: Transitional Allowance.
2. Page 97   Kailahun, Kono, and Tongo Field are towns, districts in the Eastern Province.

Chapter 13
1. Page 108   Poda Podas, Okadas: means of commercial public transport.

ABOUT THE AUTHOR

Akibo Robinson was born in Freetown, Sierra Leone, and earned a master's degree in economics from the University of Wales. He previously worked for the Commonwealth Secretariat and the United Nations, and returned to Sierra Leone in the 1990s to work with the National Commission for Social Action. Robinson is married with grown children.

Printed in Great Britain
by Amazon

34887414R00076